SECURE THE BASE

THE AFRICA LIST

SECURE THE BASE

Making Africa Visible in the Globe

NGŨGĨ WA THIONG'O

LONDON NEW YORK CALCUTTA

Series Editor
ROSALIND C. MORRIS

Seagull Books, 2016

© Ngũgĩ wa Thiong'o, 2016

ISBN 978 0 8574 2 313 9

British Library Cataloguing-in-Publication Data
A catalogue record for this book is available from the British Library.

Typeset by Seagull Books, Calcutta, India
Printed and bound by Maple Press, York, Pennsylvania, USA

CONTENTS

PREFACE

These essays are united by the concern for the place of Africa in the world today. Any discussion of the continent must take into account the depths from which Africa has emerged and the world forces—from slave trade, slavery and colonialism to debt slavery—against which it has had to struggle. A lot of good has emerged against all odds. This is a cause for hope. But such discussion must also look at what Africa has failed to do and the crimes it has brought upon itself. Central to this is the position of the ruling middle class vis-à-vis the people and the external forces. In the past, a section of this middle class has played an enabling role against the deepest interests of the continent. Even slave trade and colonialism were not without an African collaboration. Fortunately in its very midst was another section that sought alliance with the people against both the external invader and his African collaborators. The question which faced earlier generations and manifestations of the middle class is still the same: Does it see itself as accountable to the people or to the external centres of imperial power? Does it see itself as rentiers of their resources or a maker of things from their resources? Though these essays were written for diverse occasions at different times, the theme of a mimic middle class that runs away from its base among the people is one of their common threads.

Another is the question of nuclear arms. At first this may seem remote to Africa's pressing concerns. But there are urgent reasons why Africa should and must be at the forefront in calls for nuclear disarmaments and non-proliferation. It's the only continent with a moral right to do so, being the only one from where two states, South Africa and Libya, voluntarily (though no doubt under pressure) dismantled nuclear programmes. Libya even gave its nuclear material to the US for keeps. And what did Libya get in return? A nuclear-armed NATO invaded it, and turned it into a lawless state, an ironic reward for its compliance. African Union, supposedly the voice of Africa, was brushed aside with contempt. Africa's self-interest demands it have a voice in this matter of weapons of mass destruction, for, whether or not it likes, Africa has been drawn into nuclear practice and politics. France carried out its first nuclear tests in Africa;

and Israel allegedly in Prince Edward Island during the apartheid era. Africa is one of the sources of uranium, an integral component of nuclear weaponry. During the American invasion of Iraq, Niger was dragged into the controversy because of unfounded allegations that Saddam Hussein had bought uranium from it.

There is always the larger historical irony. The three leading nuclear states and nations—France, Britain and the US—have a slaving and colonial past. In a way, slavery, colonialism and nuclear armament are driven by the same instinct—contempt of other lives, particularly black lives. Although the First and Second World Wars were of European origins, Africa was drawn into them. Is there any reason to believe that Africa would not be drawn into yet another war, even if it started elsewhere?

There is also the question of survival: Africans are a part of the human race; and nuclear arms, no matter who hoards them, are a threat to humanity. 'No man is an island, entire of itself,' wrote John Donne, 'Every man is a piece of the continent, a part of the main. [. . . A]ny man's death diminishes me, because I am involved in mankind, and therefore never send to know for whom the bells tolls; it tolls for thee.'[1] Donne's call is relevant for our world today, more than when he first wrote the words, for our common planet is threatened by the man-made, profit-driven twin weapons of mass destruction—environmental crimes by the leading powers of the globe and, of course, the nuclear arms.

Although concerns for the visibility of Africa in the globe is my main concern, I wrote these essays for diverse occasions. The first essay, on the word 'tribe' in African politics, is based on the lecture I gave at the University of Hawaii, Manoa, on 28 April 2008, as the holder of the university's Dan and Maggie Inouye Distinguished Chair in Democratic Ideals. While I can understand why detractors of non-European peoples would want to append the word tribe to them, I have not been able to make sense of why African, Pacific, Native American and Indian intellectuals have embraced this pejorative term. It still baffles me why more than 40 million Yorubas are a tribe and 5 million Danes a nation! Or why non-European peoples should have the term tribesmen attached to the names of their communities and leaders. Every community has a name by which they identify themselves. Call them by that name. We talk of the English, or English people; the French, or the French people; the Chinese, or the Chinese People; the Russians, or the Russian people. Accord the same to all communities, big or small, in Africa and the world. Don't put editorial frames to their names. Just call them by the name with which they identify themselves.

The second essay, on African identities and globalization, is based on a lecture at Macalester College, St Paul, Minnesota, in 2004. The third chapter, on language and the African intellectual, was written for the Grande Finale Conference in Dakar, Senegal, on 10–12 December 2003, to mark the thirtieth anniversary of the Council for the Development of Social Science Research in Africa (CODESRIA). This is a considerably rewritten and shortened version but the essential points are the same: it's impossible to engage in any meaningful dialogue on ideas to do with Africa without, of course, raising the intellectual absurdity of the biggest continent in the world running away from its languages yet wanting to be taken seriously.

The fourth essay, on the global responsibility to protect humanity, was part of an informal interactive dialogue on the 'Responsibility to Protect' in the Trusteeship Council Chamber preceding the United Nations General Assembly debate on the same in New York on 23 July 2009. I am concerned that, under this, the West assumes that it has the responsibility to 'protect' Africa from itself. What about Africa taking the responsibility to protect and intervene in Europe and America? A really democratic and representative United Nations and Security Council would seem to be the prerequisite for any state's assumption of that responsibility. We have already seen how a noble idea, like the International Criminal Court, has been turned into an instrument, which is blind to crimes against humanity openly committed by the powerful nations while very vigilant of any in Africa. It's not that these crimes are any less, whether committed by African governments or Western ones. A Western government that sanctions torture within its borders or within rented torture chambers in other countries should be held to the same standards as governments elsewhere. It is King Lear all over again in the case of justice among and between nations: 'Through tatter'd clothes great vices do appear; / Robes and furr'd gowns hide all. Plate sin with gold, / And the strong lance of justice hurtless breaks; / Arm it in rags, a pigmy's straw does pierce it.'[2]

One of the greatest crimes against humanity was slavery which the West has never seen as anything worth apologizing for. Four hundred years of free labour is dismissed as nothing to whine about. The fifth essay, the statement on slavery, was part of an NGO briefing on 26 March 2009, occasioned by the 2009 International Day of Remembrance of the Victims of Slavery and the Transatlantic Slave Trade.

The sixth essay is based on a similar topic—the role of the intellectual in the twenty-first century—part of the President Forum of the 2005 Modern Language Association Convention in Washington DC. I could not resist an implied critique of the current conceptualization and periodization of the 'modern' and the 'postmodern'. The first explosion of a nuclear bomb in 1945 marks a clear historical ontological break with a past during which no human technology was capable of snuffing out life altogether and the beginning of a continuing present where such a technology reigns supreme. And yet this fact does not figure prominently in discussions of the constitution of the modern and postmodern, or its various post-posts. The human technology for the death of humanity is a more fundamental definition of our times than any linguistic musings and parsing of words.

The seventh essay, on writing for peace, is a fusion of musings I presented at the Interlit '82 in Cologne, I was intrigued by the fact that both countries, Germany and South Korea, once had walls dividing them, walls with origins in the Second World War and its aftermath. The wall as a barrier between nations, communities and social classes thematically sums up all the essays. The essay is driven by my continued interest in issues of peace and stability based on equality of peoples and nations.

Underlying all the essays is a call for a visionary, united African leadership to secure the continent and its resources and take responsibility of its future. Africa, endowed with enormous human and natural resources, is the biggest continent. Its encirclement—its being denied a seat in the United Nations Security Council, its being defined in terms of North and South of the Sahara, then into Europhone zones (Franco-, Anglo-, Luso-Hispa-), its being free for all external forces to intervene—has everything to do with that fact. Keep Africa eternally weak, eternally divided, eternally fighting religious wars, eternally buying weapons of war, eternally using the military against African populations, eternally assuming that the West, Europe in particular, is heaven. The fact is, for the last 400 years, Europe and the West have been Africa's hell, with Africa a European heaven. Africa must become Africa's heaven. But it is only Africa that can realize this for itself, lift itself into being a respected player in the world. It must rediscover and affirm self-pride, first by respecting the lives of the least among us. Respect the African body. For this, the African leadership, a new one, I hope, must stop the business of making Africa the eternal donor to the West, and relate to the world on the basis of reciprocity—equal give-and-take. Even within capitalist assumptions, the way to go is to develop an intra-Africa common market which calls for intra-African communications—village to village, town to town, region to region, east, west, north and south. The challenge is to make African diversity in languages, culture and religions a strength, not a weakness. It's only a united Africa and a vision of tomorrow that can bring about its visibility. The new Africa must be reflected in Africa's place in the world.

This new assertive Africa will also make its voice known all over the globe when it comes to the treatment of peoples of African origins, wherever in the world they be. When black people in the US, South America, Europe, Asia and the Middle East are hunted down or mistreated, the renascent Africa must be able to come to their defence. Marcus Garvey used to call for an Africa for Africans, at home and abroad. Making Africa visible in the world, by first securing our base, will be an important step towards that dream.

Notes

1 John Donne, 'Meditation XVII' (available at: http://-www.online-literature.com/donne/409/; last accessed on 16 April 2015).

2 William Shakespeare, *King Lear* in *Complete Works* (W. J. Craig ed.) (Oxford: Oxford University Press, 1943), 4.6.169–72, p. 935.

CONTEMPT AND SELF-CONTEMPT

*How the Word 'Tribe' Obscures
the Reality of African Politics*

At the heart of the democratic or any political process in society is the question of power. In fact, we can define politics simply as the organization of power in society. Who or what social group holds power? For whom does it exercise that power? What are the values or social goals—economic, political, cultural and even psychological—to which that power is exercised? The questions are valid for the system of laws and norms within nations, namely, internal relations as well as for those that govern relations between nations, namely, international relations.

Those same questions underlie the Lincolnian definition of democracy as the government of the people, by the people, for the people. In some ways, the most important elements in that definition are the three tiny connective prepositions: 'of', 'by' and 'for'. For the Lincolnian definition to apply, the three prepositions must be in place. Many governments and states, including the home of Abraham Lincoln, the United States of America, fall short of the Lincolnian democratic ideal because they leave out one or more of those prepositions. Which prepositions are emphasized, left out or followed through affects the ends for which power is exercised.

The value towards which power is exercised and how is a moral and ethical question. Laws are the instruments chosen by society for the proper control and exercise of power to ensure that they meet those ends embedded in their formulation. Law is a rule, a statement of *oughtness*, but, in contrast to other rules, law has a coercive component, the tools that ensure compliance. The 'thou shalt not kill' of the biblical Ten Commandments is different from the 'you must not kill' of the largely secular jurisprudence, because the latter spells out clearly the enforceable consequences of its infringement. The statement of a rule, its application and its coercive component raise moral issues involving, for instance, the congruence of law—or lack thereof—with justice, and the moral limits of the use of the coercive component of law, such as the use of torture to extract information from a citizen. So, no matter what angle we take, the questions of power in society, even within a democratic framework, come back to those of morality.

Not surprisingly, the words by which a certain law is formulated are the subject of debates on their use and interpretation. The exercise of democratic ideals—or the statement of law and its application—within and between nations is often conditioned by our self-perception and our perception of others; and these are often conditioned by definitions of words. For instance, democracy in ancient Athens was actually direct democracy, where every citizen of the *polis* was able to cast his vote on matters of war and peace. Direct democracy, as opposed to representative democracy, is an excellent ideal. But that same democracy was predicated on the alleged fact that women, slaves and foreigners—'barbarians', as they were called—were not citizens. The word citizen determines inclusion or exclusion. The American Declaration of Independence talked glowingly in almost Rousseauian *Social Contract* terms about the fact that people were created equal and endowed by their creator with certain inalienable rights, but excluded black people and women from the category of 'people'. In war, certain word usages can dehumanize the other—Commies, Viet Congs, capitalist pigs and so on—and hence remove any moral scruples in dealing with them. Words become very important in the power relations between individuals and groups, in the exercise of law and democratic ideals. Quite often, they define and even erase the individuality of a member of a group by their religious, racial, gender or biological markers or affiliations.

A good example is the use of the five-letter English word tribe. The mainstream Western media's analysis of events in Africa reveals the word as the main obstacle in the way of a meaningful illumination of dynamics in modern Africa. Tribe—with its clearly pejorative connotation of the primitive and the pre-modern—is contrasted with nation which connotes a more positive sense of arrival at the modern. In much of the media coverage of Africa, every African community is said to comprise a tribe and every African a tribesman. We can see the absurdity of the current usages, where a group of 300,000 Icelanders constitutes a nation while 30 million Ibos make up a tribe. And yet, looked at through more objective lenses, what's commonly described as a tribe fulfils all the criteria of shared history, geography, economic life, language and culture that are used to define a nation. These critical attributes are clearly social and historical, not biological.

Nonetheless, to the analysts, tribe is like a genetic stamp on every African character, explaining his every utterance and action, particularly vis-à-vis other African communities. Using the same template of Tribe X versus Tribe Y, print and electronic media and even progressive thinkers often simply look at the ethnic origins of the leading actors in a conflict and immediately place them in the category of X or Y. So, whatever the crisis, in whichever part of Africa, at whichever time in history, the analysts arrive at one explanation: it is all because of the traditional enmity between Tribe X and Tribe Y. It is like looking at John McCain, seeing that he was born in a naval base in Panama; then looking at Barack Obama, seeing that he was born in Hawaii; and then concluding that their political differences are due to the places of their birth or that their differences are rooted in an assumed traditional enmity between those born on a naval base and those on an island.

This template of Tribe X versus Tribe Y dominated discussions of the 2007 political crisis in Kenya, framing it in terms of the Luo and the Gĩkũyũ, simply because Raila Odinga, then the opposition leader, later prime minister (2008–13), was Luo, and Mwai Kibaki, the president (2002–13), was Gĩkũyũ. What did not fit into that neat composition was often glossed over. For instance, Gĩkũyũ and the Luo people never shared boundaries, so the claim that they could have been traditional enemies defeats reason and common sense. But analysts were undaunted in their persistent use of the formula. Even the fact that the two leaders had followers across other communities, or the fact that much of the gruesome anti-Gĩkũyũ ethnic cleansing came largely from Eldoret North, a Kalenjin area, and Narok, an area under Maasai dominance, was ignored in order not to muddy the waters of the familiar formula.

Many newspapers talked of a continuous Gĩkũyũ dominance in economics and politics ont only throughout the 45 years of Independence but also before. The British ruled Kenya as a white settler colonial state for 60 years, from about 1895 to 1963. Jomo Kenyatta, a Gĩkũyũ, ruled for 15 years, from 1963 to 1978. Daniel arap Moi, a Kalenjin, not a Gĩkũyũ, ruled for the next 24, from 1978 to 2002. Yet the discussions on events unfolding in Kenya rarely mentioned the 60 years of British settler rule or the 24 years of Moi (not Kalenjin) dictatorship. The media and experts on Kenya developed a strange amnesia, yanking the years of Moi dictatorship off the pages of Kenyan postcolonial history—the better to have a narrative of Luo versus Gĩkũyũ, or one of an uninterrupted Gĩkũyũ dominance and privilege.

This does not mean that different African communities, whether now or earlier, have not harboured animosity towards one another. In fact, the various precolonial African communities fought over disputed property and territory and engaged in wars of conquest and domination. The vaunted empires of Ghana, Mali, Zulu and Ashanti were built on conquest and maintained through systems of subjugation and tutelage. But there were also long periods when those same groups' relationships with one another were characterized by peace and commerce. In this, there is nothing peculiarly African. All relationships between communities in history have alternated between hostility and hospitality. Whatever else may have been the case, these communities did not see themselves as living for the sole purpose of waging war.

It is fair to say that 'tribe', 'tribalism' and 'tribal wars', the terms so often used to explain conflict in Africa, were colonial inventions. Most African languages do not have the equivalent of the English word tribe, with its pejorative connotations that sprung up in the evolution of the anthropological vocabulary of eighteenth- and nineteenth-century European adventurism in Africa. The words have companionship with other colonial conceptions, such as 'primitive', the 'Dark Continent', 'backward races' and 'warrior communities'.

In slave and colonial conquests, Europeans would ally with one African community to subjugate another, not in the interest of the African ally but in their own imperial interests. Of course, it is the case that precolonial wars regularly entailed the abduction of women into both slavery and enforced marriages, but in most cases there were rules governing warfare. There is no way of prettifying war between two or three human communities. But the fact remains that there is no colonial story anywhere which does not contain grim episodes of wanton massacres of men, women and children. Historian David Stannard documents incidents of genocidal practices against native peoples in his book *American Holocaust* (1992). But there are many other colonial genocides in the hands of virtually every colonial power. Such genocidal practices are preceded by demonization and dehumanization through words. Sometimes, the ally who helped to subjugate the neighbouring communities was later turned into a conquered subject and made to live in the same territory with the communities they had helped to conquer. Colonial states deliberately kept the colonized peoples in perpetual tension through the well-known imperial tradition of divide and rule, the Roman *Divide at Impere*.

Often, the colonial state would use one community as the source of the army, another as the source of the police and yet another as the source of labour, while others were kept as 'tribal' specimens of the primitive, a living museum of the true 'cultural' African, with his spear and animal skin. From all the communities would also come a small pool of intellectual labour: Africans educated in the colonial-government and missionary schools became junior cadres of the colonial administration and the Christian enterprise. Over time, the cumulative effects of these policies and practices stoked and deepened bitterness not towards the colonial state but often towards one another, with the colonizer presenting himself as the neutral arbiter between the 'eternally' hostile communities. A rationale often used to defend colonialism was that the imperial conquerors had stopped 'tribal' wars.

The clash between Africa and Europe in the colonizing process was essentially one between the advanced capitalism of the time and precapitalist peasant economies. A hallmark of capitalism, especially colonial capitalism, is uneven regional development. With extraction of minerals and the development of mono-crop economies—thus turning arable land from food production to the cultivation of coffee, tea, sisal and cocoa as raw materials for export—the colonial economy served and complemented the economy of the colonizing country. While the colony as a whole served the metropolitan imperial centre with raw materials, the rural areas within it served the towns with labour and food supply. Towns and cities were, of course, the hubs of capitalist activity. The regions around them gained from improved infrastructure and access to market and other facilities, however limited the access and the returns.

But capitalist enterprise also deepened uneven social development, especially in regions that were the sources of labour. An underpaid working class, often divorced from the soil, emerged from those communities. What also emerged was a middle class that gained from the fallouts of capitalist enterprise and colonial administration. So, to the problem of uneven regional development was added to that of uneven social development within each region.

Since regions coincided with linguistic communities, uneven regional and social development affected the communities differently. Naturally, this deepened divisions within and between communities. Anticolonial resistance movements generally tried to bridge the gaps within and between these communities. A social vision of a different future of freedom, democracy and economic welfare helped to forge a national consciousness.

But the colonial state was always on the lookout against any positive rapprochements between communities. In Kenya, for instance, the British settler state would not allow the formation of a nationwide social or political organization among Africans. European settlers, and even Asian immigrants, could organize nationally, but Africans were allowed to organize labour, social and political unions only within ethnic boundaries. The divisive tactics of the colonial regime reached their peak during the armed struggle waged by the Land and Freedom Army (Mau Mau) from 1952 to 1960, when Africans could form parties only along district lines. It was not until 1960, barely three years before Independence, that the colonial state permitted nationwide political parties.

Taken as a whole, these measures and practices encouraged ethnic consciousness; the 'biological system' they came to call 'tribalism' derived, of course, from the conception of the tribe as a monolithic genetic entity. The result of the history and usage of this one English word, tribe, have had negative effects on the evaluation and self-evaluation of Africa, for African intellectuals have internalized this divisive inheritance of colonialism. They have come to see one another through the colonial invention of the tribe, tribalism and tribal wars, elevating cultural marks of difference such as distinct rituals, and even languages, as the real basis of divisions and communal identity. The subtext is clear: leave all reason at the door before you enter the chamber of African conflicts.

To explain problems in terms of the biological make-up of the characters is to express social despair, for if a problem is biological, its solution can only be biological. Let's put it another way. If a problem is seen as biological, then the solution through social and political means appears nearly impossible. All of this has coalesced into indifference to African lives by the international and national middle classes. This attitude may explain, in part, why people—including Africans—can watch genocide in Rwanda and Darfur and not feel the urgency to act, as if they were waiting for biology to sort itself out. Political dictatorships—most even sponsored by the West— emerge, and people shrug their shoulders, eliciting the unspoken or spoken view: tribal mentality—so difficult to penetrate. As for the African middle class, self-hatred from years of internalizing the colonial gaze makes some among them gleeful at the humiliation of another African. Political mismanagement as a negation of democratic and social rights is altogether ignored, and ethnic cleansing, the negation of the basic human right to life, is tolerated. But African problems, like those of any other peoples in history, have economic, political and social roots. They arise historically, not biologically.

Some years ago, I wrote that there are only two 'tribes' in Africa, the Haves and the Have-Nots, and these are to be found in all communities in varying degrees of intensity. But the Haves of one community tend to point to the Haves of another community as the only Haves, or label an entire community as the Have-It-Alls. Political warlords, often millionaires, then emerge as the defenders of the community against the enemy community of Haves. This allows political warlords to talk about ethnic purity as the key to economic and political liberation. These warlords often make sweetheart deals with Western companies—or are promised such deals, should they ever come to power. The Congo provides the best example: even in the so-called tribal wars—that is, among the political warlords—there is always the outsider who wants to see what he can pick from the ruins. So I should note the real existence of a third tribe: the Corporate Tribe of the West.

In the case of Kenya, one would have thought that a look at the underlying problems, colonial legacies, uneven development, the deepening and widening gap between the rich and the poor, weak democratic institutions, the devastation of the national psyche by 20 years of a West-backed Moi dictatorship, and the continuous dominance of Western interests, would have ruined the neat narrative of Tribe X versus Tribe Y. Or that it might have made us see that there were lessons the world could learn from the Kenyan crisis—for instance, that a fair economic playground within and between nations is important for the exercise of democratic ideals. But seeing Africa in terms of non-rational mystical terms such as tribe and tribalism prevents people from seeing Africa's problems as a part of global concerns. And yet, the basic roots of instability in Africa are clearly the same as those that underlie a much broader instability today, in the era of globalization.

The world today is characterized by two rifts that deepen and widen daily. First, the rift between the wealth of a group of largely Western nations and a majority of poor nations, primarily in Africa, Asia and Latin America. As it is depicted by one of the characters in my novel *Wizard of the Crow* (2006), this is the rift between the givers and recipients of charity, between credit or donor nations and beggar or debt-burdened nations. And yet, the natural resources of the debtor nations feed the creditor nations. Second, the rift within each and every nation in the world where a small social stratum stands on mass poverty below. Within these nations, the beggars and the homeless multiply; prisons harbour millions who could easily constitute a nation, were they living in a territory all their own. And they call this development.

My contention is that these rifts between and within nations constitute the roots of great instability in today's world. Democratic ideals must come to terms with economic ideals for the political and cultural empowerment of the weakest among us. What is needed is not mysticism but, rather, rational analysis of social situations—in Africa and elsewhere. One cannot give high marks for the development of nation on the basis of a hundred millionaires who stand on the shoulders of a hundred million beggars. Progress and development need to be measured from the standpoint of the quality of life of those at the bottom of the mountain and not those at the top. Only then will reason, law and democratic ideals be in accord with the demands of social justice.

PRIVATIZE OR BE DAMNED

*Africa, Globalization
and Capitalist Fundamentalism*

The world in which Africa tries to find its place is one of contradictions. Technology and human ingenuity have opened an endless frontier in outer and internal space, even decoding the key to life; yet human greed has decreed that there be poverty and disease on earth. Technology offers the possibility of plenty. Profit motivates human ingenuity to create scarcity. The means to salvage life is demeaned by the means to savage it. Weapons of mass destruction, no matter which nation hoards them, are the sword of Damocles over the masses of the globe, including the nation that holds them; they cannot guarantee security between or within nations—only false peace, regional conflicts and strife that still end in threats of war and more wars. Anxiety and insecurity haunt the streets of all, even the most heavily armed nation. The prison population is the most rapidly growing demographic in the poorest and wealthiest nations alike. The splendour-in-squalor character of our globe is at the heart of the complex contradictions of globalization.

Where is Africa's place in this scenario? What is Africa in the global space? Every phenomenon in nature, society and thought, including the character of its being, is affected by the external and internal dynamics of its being and becoming. African development is no exception. The Cold War of superpower rivalries affected the character of the postcolonial state that emerged in the 1960s. The military and civilian dictatorships, while feeding on the fertile soil of weak democratic and economic bases within, were also a function of superpower rivalries, with African regions often fighting proxy wars that provided nothing more than killing fields to test the effectiveness of rival armaments. The struggles for democracy by a broad social movement and the end of the Cold War saw the liberalization of the internal space, with many more African leaders willing to retire, instead of being retired by death through old age or military coups. These are positive internal developments.

But just as decolonization took place under conditions of the Cold War, which left its mark, these post–Cold War developments are taking place under conditions of intensified *economic* globalization. Not that globalization is a new phenomenon. It has been a feature of capital since its genesis in the sixteenth century, challenging and later replacing feudalism as the dominant and determining force in social and economic production. Explorations and colonial ventures are concomitant with its genesis. Following from Adam Smith, Karl Marx observed that the rosy dawn of the era of capitalist production was signalled by 'the discovery of gold and silver in America, the uprooting, enslavement and entombment in the mines of the aboriginal population, the beginning of the conquest and looting of the East Indies, the turning of Africa into a warren for the commercialized hunting of black skins'.[1] The 'rosy dawn' was the mercantile phase of capital that fuelled and was fuelled by the slave trade and created slave plantations, the totality resulting in accumulation that permitted the mercantile phase to metamorphose into the industrial one. In his book *Capitalism and Slavery* (1944), Eric Williams has ably documented the connection between the slave trade, the plantations and the rise of industrial capitalism to dominance. The industrial phase of nineteenth-century capitalism drove the scramble for colonies as sources of raw materials and markets for finished goods. Military invasions and conquests, under the self-serving ideals of pacification and enlightenment, integrated Africa into the capitalist order. The European bourgeoisie set out to build heaven on hell in Africa, and, in an orgy of reckless iconoclasm, destroyed the old gods that did not recognize the system of heaven for a few on a hell for the many. In *The Communist Manifesto* (1848), Marx and Engels predicted the worldwide character of this development when they spoke of the bourgeoisie, through its exploitation of the world market, giving a cosmopolitan character to production and consumption in every country. It dislodged old established national industries with new ones utilizing raw materials drawn from the remotest zones—industries whose products were consumed not only at home but also in every quarter of the globe.[2] The industrial soon transformed itself into finance capital; money that previously enabled exchange became a commodity of the highest order, a laser-guided missile that sped up capitulation and crumbled the protective walls of nations. The global dominance of finance capital was foreseen by both Lenin, in his book *Imperialism: The Highest Stage of Capitalism* (1917), published at the beginning of the First World War, and the Bretton Woods Agreement, which was worked out at the end of the Second World War and which resulted in the creation of the World Bank, the International Monetary Fund (IMF), and the General Agreement on Trade and Tariffs (GATT).[3] The very titles of the Bretton Woods institutions signal the globe as the theatre for the actions of finance capital.

Though adversely so, Africa has always been an integral part of the key moments in the evolution of the globalizing tendency of capital. The mercantile moment gave Africa slavery; the industrial, colonialism; and the finance, neocolonialism, the heart of globalization.

Globalization today, then, is the maturing of a tendency and process inherent in capitalism. However, if globalization has been the tendency and context of the process of capitalist modernity, there is a difference between its pre– and post–Cold War manifestations. The earlier phases and forms paid homage to the notion of laissez-faire at least, even when the inevitable monopolies were telling a different story. Free competition assumes different paths towards capitalist paradise. What characterizes globalization in its current form is the ideological and practical imperative of capitalist fundamentalism.

Fundamentalism—economic, political or religious —is, essentially, an insistence that there is only one way of organizing reality. Margaret Thatcher's often cited phrase 'There Is No Alternative' (TINA)[4] best illustrates this in relation to politics and economy, but it embodies the same reductionism as does religious fundamentalism. There is only one God, his name is market, and the West is his only guardian. Enter ye and throw your fate at the tender mercies of the market. In reality, the tender mercies are belied by the invisible writing on the wall: 'Lasciate Ogne sperenca voi ch'intrate'—abandon all hope all ye who enter here. The voices of those who might see the writing on the wall are drowned by the calls for the worship of the market, literally, with the common credo of privatization, reducible to a maxim: Privatize or Perish. If a nation deviates from the ordained path, for instance, by questioning the disciplinary mechanisms of 'aid' conditions or failing to privatize public enterprises and introduce narrowly defined forms of liberal democracy, then it faces excommunication from the global capitalist temple and expulsion into purgatory. Julius Nyerere's Tanzania of the 1980s was brought to its knees for questioning neoliberal doctrine. Even previously compliant dictators were not immune from punishment when they tried to retain parastatals, punished not because these were sources of looting and patronage but because they were semi-publicly owned. The ones that earned heavenly wrath, even in the Western and later Eastern Europe, were public institutions that seemed to work. Where possible, they were dismantled and sold to private hands. Even the Conservative Harold Macmillan was to flinch at the reckless speed at which his conservative successor Margaret Thatcher went about selling the profitable publicly owned institutions to private hands at throw-away prices. The publicly owned institutions left standing were those that did not shine: they were left alone as negative examples, the grimy face of the publicly owned.

This radical turn, then, conceptualizes capitalism as a religious system, with the market as the mediating deity in the conflicting claims of its adherents. The market is the supreme deity guarded by a band of armed angels, apostles and priests who assign Hell for the unrepentant sinner, Purgatory for those showing signs of repentance and Paradise for the saved. It is Dante's sytsem of Hell whose consequences I tried to explore in my novel *Wizard of the Crow*.

Unfortunately, the consequences are not fictional —they are direly real for the political economies of peripheral capitalist societies, such as those in Africa, who have been forced to turn public social goods, including education, health and water, into sacrificial offerings for the market. This has added havoc to the farmer already hit hard by the discriminatory policies of the World Trade Organization (WTO), the successor to GATT, especially in the area of agrarian subsidies.[5] These societies are under constant surveillance to ensure they don't sin by breaking any of the market commandments, the first of which is: Get the dirty hands of the state off the economy. It's ironic that those who insist that the state has no role in the economy are the first to seize the state to make it serve capital against labour, the private against the public. The fact is, in a class-structured society, the state is never neutral and, depending on which social class (and race and gender and even religion) controls it, it plays a decisive role in the direction of the economy and the social ends to which the wealth of the nation is put.

With the insistence that there is only one way of organizing an economy, capitalist fundamentalism is already challenging the traditional attributes of the nation-state, such as its assumed right to formulate national economic policies. The IMF makes Third World economic policies; in some cases, the august body has offices in the ministries of finance and economic planning, quite often having a say in the appointment of key civil servants as overseers of the national treasury. A state that has to have its economic policies approved by another has already surrendered some of its sovereignty to the approving overseer. Rapid developments in information technology, with the Internet drawing the world into one web, further erode the nation-state's control of what is within its territory, for no state can now effectively contain the flow and exchange of information across national borders.

Even the state's role as the provider for social needs and the employer of intellectuals has been usurped, this time by the non-governmental organizations (NGOs), the secular missionary societies in the era of globalization, not too dissimilar to the role of Christian missions in the era of colonization and colonial rule. What characterized the nineteenth-century expansion of capitalism—its rush for colonies and the ceding of territories to companies like the Imperial East African Company—was paralleled by the rise and expansion of missionary societies which also carved spaces among themselves, even within the same colonial territory. Though clearly part of the same colonial enterprise, and assuming protection from the colonial state, they also sometimes acted in competition with the state. The missionary societies provided many social services, including education and medicine. (Mongo Beti's *The Poor Christ of Bomba* [1971] dramatizes this sibling rivalry between the missionary and the colonial administrator.)

Foreign NGOs today are similarly allocating spaces to themselves and posing as if they are on the side of the people against both the postcolonial state and their financial sponsor, the foreign state. Yet they are funded by the treasuries of their governments, mostly Western.[6] They are an arm of the foreign policy of the bankrolling states. The local NGOs they work or partner with are genuinely non-governmental—they don't get a cent from their governments. But the local NGOs often get their financial support from the very foreign NGOs that are funded by their own government treasuries. Many products of national universities compete for consultancy by constituting themselves as NGOs or playing advisory role to the foreign NGO. The products of the hard work of these native consultants, even the tone of the language in which their critiques and reports are written, are often within the broad consensus of the sources of funds. A native NGO that may call for the change of a corrupt, West-supported regime or call on the nation-state to challenge capitalist fundamentalism may find that its funding has dwindled overnight. He who pays the piper calls the tune, if not the lyrics, the tone and, in this case, the payers are unrepentant disciples of capital. However, just like the religious missionaries of yesterday, some of these secular missionaries do often deliver much-needed services.

The ascendancy of finance capital affects other areas of Africa's social life, including the conception of politics in general and democracy in particular. Thus, what is often touted as West-supported 'freedom' and democracy are essentially the freedom and democracy of finance capital to go in and out of national boundaries without the interference of the nation-state. But does that mean that this capital is genuinely supranational? Are we talking of a homeless capital? Not really, for, while claiming the globe as its playground, its base is still in the national homelands of what largely goes under the name of the West, mainly the Euro-American sector of the West. It may roam the globe, bringing down the walls of other nation-states, but it knows where to return with its profits. The case of China brings out the irony of capital invested by a one-party state, but African states that have bought into the gospel of privatization won't see their role as providing an enabling environment for corporate capital.

Often, these states compete among themselves to prove which is best able to deliver a cheap, submissive labour force and protect the free trade zones that are off limits for the laws of the country. The result of this process for Africa and many countries around the globe is a state too weak to interfere with the operation of finance capital but strong enough to contain the population should they rise against the ensuing social depredation. It's easy to see why and how.

Instability is the name of the myopic state. In acting as an overseer of free operations of foreign finance capital, unable to deliver even a modicum of social services, unable to guarantee decent minimal housing, health and education, the postcolonial state's hold on the allegiance of the population is considerably weakened. The citizens view the state with suspicion, as an enemy of the people (which it often is), and their gratitude to NGOs may make them see imperialist nations as their allies against the repressive practices of their own state. The irony is, of course, that the generous NGOs and the local state—rivals for the gratitude and allegiance of the people—are armed by the same Western sources. The state is armed with lethal weapons; the NGO with food coupons.

In order to create even a modicum of stability, such a postcolonial state will rely on police boots and military bayonets—a return, ironically, to the character of the Cold War–era postcolonial state, and even further back in time, to that of the colonial state. Thus, the emerging post–Cold War state, initially wearing the loosely fitting robes of democracy, is turned into its opposite: a policing state without the capacity and the means to speak for the nation, even on the moral matter of national pride. In Daniel arap Moi's Kenya, schoolchildren sang praises to the leader because in times of famine, a result of his close cohorts selling off surplus grain, he went to the US and came back with yellow corn and loans for buying arms from the US. Begging became a desirable ideal and the leader became the number-one beggar with all the self-effacement that goes with begging bowls in Western capitals.

The two gaps of wealth and poverty *between* and *within* nations, rooted in the economic practice of global-ization, are rapidly widening, and herein lies the great

paradox where production is clearly global but the appropriation of the product is unmistakably private: globalize
production, regionalize profiteering, privatize it. The
neologisms of outsourcing, that is, take production where
labour is cheapest, and insourcing, that is, bring back the
profit (or production in the event of instability out there),
testify to this. The private disposal of the public proposal
adds to the paradox referred to at the beginning of the
essay: that despite the enormous power of new technologies brought forth by the globalization of the division of
labour, the result is the globalization of poverty. Nurture,
which could tame the vicissitudes of nature, breeds
greater social vicissitudes. The deepening discrepancy
between the have and have-not conditions of an increasingly globalized world is a foundation for new types of
authoritarianism. It's a vicious circle: capitalist market
fundamentalism generates instability everywhere; the
instability generates fundamentalisms in alliance[7] or
opposition. Is it any surprise that the era of capitalist fundamentalism, what some scholars dub neoliberalism,
which begins, roughly, with Ronald Reagan, Margaret
Thatcher and Helmut Kohl (though the threesome did
not create it), has seen the rise of unmitigated religious
fundamentalism—Christian, Islamic, Jewish and Hindu?

II

Unfortunately, Africa fares the worst, despite or because of the fact that the continent has always been a player in the development of the modern capitalist world. Each moment in the journey of capital has Africa as a captive. Under the slave trade, the African body becomes a commodity. Under the ensuing slave plantation system, Africa supplies unpaid labour that works the sugar and cotton fields. Under colonialism, Africa supplies raw materials—gold, diamonds, copper, uranium, coffee and cocoa—without having control over the prices.[8] Under the new global situation of debts, debt servicing and conditionality, Africa is weighed down by debt slavery. Just as Africa became a net exporter of the labour it most needed for its own development and the net exporter of minerals and raw materials it most needed for its own development, today, under debt slavery, Africa becomes a net exporter of the very capital it most needs. Africa, endowed with all the resources of nature, becomes the land most bowed down by the man-wrought ills of poverty, disease and ignorance. In relation to Africa, slavery is the continuous theme in the journey of capital: the plantation dissolving into colonial rule dissolving into debt slavery.

How does Africa get itself out of this quagmire and transform itself into an equal player in the world—an equal giver and an equal recipient? How can it relate to other regions on the basis of equality and mutual respect?

Given the fact that the globe is *one* and its resources are not endlessly renewable, how does Africa obtain its fair share?

First, Africa must resist seduction into slumber by the Western self-image of an endlessly generous and patient donor. Indeed, Africa has to stop acting the grateful beggar to the charitable West. One need only delve into the archives of European and American libraries and catalogue the ills the West has visited on Africa to see that the present state of the continent can be blamed on the dastardly history of the imperial West. But Africa cannot lay back and wait for the West to realize the harm it has done and repent. Does anyone expect that Europe, while running the slave and the colonial system, would have behaved differently? Nor should anyone, under the current wave of globalization, expect the West to come forward, kneel before Africa and say: 'We have wronged you, we have stolen from you. Forgive us our trespasses, and, by the way, here are reparations, a token of our repentance.'

Africa's awakening must be two-pronged: Africa must not let the West off the moral hook. The continent has to intensify its demands for social justice and the rectification of glaring historical injustices. The West must be made to accept its responsibility for crimes against African humanity. Nineteenth-century abolitionist Frederick Douglass once said that power concedes nothing without demand. It never has and it never will. This is true of power within a nation and among nations. Africa's own history tells us that every gain—and there have been many—has been as a result of struggles. Africa did not get freedom from slavery and colonialism on a silver platter. It came from resistance, as a result of demand.

Demands that have a chance of winning cannot be made from a position of weakness. Power has never conceded to weakness. Africa must not wait to get itself out of the quagmire through reparations willingly dished out by the very forces that gain from its weak position. Nor can Africa afford to sit back and blame. Instead, Africa has to lift itself into power from where it can make demands.

Hence the other prong. The starting point must be a thorough self-examination. While conceding that the way out of its historical nightmare is beset with major structural obstacles, Africa must be proactive even within its marginality in the global capitalist system. Although not under conditions of its own choice, for instance, the current relentless drive of capitalist fundamentalism, Africa must strive to seize back its agency and write its own history. Not to do so would be to surrender to the fatalism inherent in Western TINA-ism, and a major dishonour to Africa's collective memory of resistance in all the previous phases of globalization. For Africa, it should never be a case of the state leaving the economic matters to the tender mercies of a mindless market but, rather, to make it genuine people's states. Currently, African states are owned by a group of comprador bourgeoisies intent on looting their nations. They use the state to create a looter's paradise. The different factions of the comprador wear ethnic colours to fight for ascendancy of their faction in the looting spree.

A struggle that does not make an inventory of what it can do for itself, and then rely on that as its starting point, is doomed to fail. Thus, taking stock of its own weaknesses and strengths should be the beginning of any organized proactivism. Were Africa to examine its history seriously, the continent could learn useful lessons for the present. The most successful struggles, including those of the Haitian Africans in 1789 and the Mau Mau in the Kenya of the 1950s, were based on self-reliance and a belief in their capacity to change the world. However weak it may now appear to itself, Africa has to take Nyerere's credo of self-reliance seriously. A belief in self is the beginning of strength.

The critical look at self must begin with a profound questioning of the assumption that the middle class is the means, object and measure of progress and development. From Asia to Africa to South America, a prosperous middle class, a global middle class, with shared values and lifestyles, is currently being touted as exactly that. It does not matter that millions of working people—the worker, the small farmer—are sinking in misery. The splendour of the middle class blinds us to the squalor of the working class. The very visibility of the middle and upper classes makes the poverty of the working and the underclass invisible.

The history of the modern African middle class has both gory and glorious sides. During the period of the slave trade, elements of this class, or its nascent equivalent, collaborated with European traders in aiding the sale of fellow Africans. It was not European armies that raided and caught slaves; rather, armies of one ethnicity attacked another to capture slaves and then exchanged them for glittering trinkets manufactured in Europe. During colonialism, a section of the same class collaborated with the colonial state and became the slave driver of the colonial plantations. This section included the *colonial* armies and police force which would hunt down anticolonial nationalists, and which, on the eve of Independence, miraculously transformed into *national* armies and police forces carrying aloft the banner of Independence, its bands leading the national anthem. Even the colour of the uniforms did not change; only the labels on shirt flaps and caps did.

The glorious side tried to bring the different ethnic communities together to gain strength from a unity of numbers and vision; they led the resistance against slave raids and the trade in human beings, and against colonial domination. While a Mobutu was elevated to the rank of colonel (or whatever) and proudly carried the Belgian flag in the colonial army, a Lumumba was languishing in prison, crying freedom. To every Mobutu, there was a

Lumumba; every Buthelezi, a Mandela; and every Afrifa–Kotoka, a Kwame Nkrumah.

Africa must question the problematic relationship of the national middle class to the imperialist bourgeoisie on the one hand and to the people on the other. In *The Wretched of the Earth* (1961), Frantz Fanon sees this relationship as the location of Africa's weakness and strength, depending on which relationship is dominant at any moment in history. Fanon describes the national bourgeoisie that leads the anticolonial resistance and obtains power as an underdeveloped middle class with no economic muscle, counting neither financiers nor industrialists among its ranks. It is not engaged in production, invention, building or labour. It is completely canalized into intermediary activities. It has no arms, no guns and no armoured vehicles.

That being the case, whence did it get the power to challenge the armed might of the colonial state? It is only through its relationship with the people. It organized the working people, the small farmers, fisher folk, herds people, the landless and the jobless, factory and plantation workers. It worked with their dreams for better wages, better returns for their crops, adequate schools, affordable houses and healthy bodies. Indeed, it facilitated people's dreams for the power to change the conditions of their lives. The nationalist middle class put its resources—its knowledge of the world, books and ideas—at the disposal of the struggle. In the South Africa of the late nineteenth and early twentieth centuries, the ideas of Booker T. Washington, W. E. B. Du Bois, Marcus Garvey, Karl Marx and even those emanating from different religious movements (the idea of independent churches, for instance) were seriously debated, with the intellectuals, through newspapers and books, trying to pass on the ideas to the people in their own languages. In the Kenya of the 1920s and 30s, the intellectuals who came across Garvey's newspaper *Negro World* shared what they read with those who could not access it. This intellectual class had an organic relationship with the masses.

At the national territorial level, it championed national unity against the divide-and-rule tactics of the colonial regime. At the continental level, it came up with the vision of pan-Africanism that embraced those who live on the continent and in diaspora. Their pan-Africanism discounted the colonial game of dividing continent into Saharan and sub-Saharan Africa and rejected regional phonic identities arising from their colonial relationship to major European powers. At the international level, the anticolonial struggle was consistent in its characterization of the enemy as imperialist rule on behalf of the international class that owned the mines and plantations, the manufacturing industries and the banks—in other words, the rule that helped the imperialist bourgeoisie gain from the miserable conditions of the poorly paid labour force. The intellectuals of the anticolonial section of the middle class armed themselves with a positive sense of themselves and their place in history. Their vision of being was anchored in the people, the real power base of the successful anti-colonial resistance against imperialism.

You would think that this relationship, which had resulted in triumph against all the armed odds, would be the rock-bottom foundation of the postcolonial state. But this expectation was defeated.

When the nationalist middle class took over the state, it changed its relationship with the people. It refused to see that its power did not come from its ownership of the levers of the economy—for it simply did not; the inter-national bourgeoisie still owned these. With the pride of a peacock, the nationalist middle class began to behave as if its beautiful colours came from its cozy relationship with imperialism. It was as if it had, after all, been handed power on a silver platter.

Fanon argues, in the brilliant chapter titled 'The Pitfalls of National Consciousness', that its new mission had nothing to do with transforming the nation: '[I]ts vocation is not to transform the nation but prosaically serve as a conveyor belt for capitalism,'[9] under the mask of neocolonialism. According to Fanon, even in the days when nationalization was a magic word, this class only nationalized and normalized the unfair advantages that were a legacy of the colonial period. The classic enact-ment of this once occurred at a public meeting in which Jomo Kenyatta, newly installed as the president of a nation that had fought for its Independence, castigated those nationalist leaders who refused to grab land from the masses as lazy, extolling the hard work of those that had become rich overnight. Others who later wrote that political without economic independence would just remain a flag blowing in the wind were cast into prison. The other classic case was that of the Ghanaian minister who bought a golden bed in England with public funds—a mockery of Nkrumah's call for austerity.

The economic consequences were dire not because the people stopped producing but because the structures that bound them to the international capitalist order as extensions of European economies never really changed. It was a case of the same old white wine in new bottles. In Kenya, there was not a single new railroad since the one laid by the colonial state at the beginning of the colonial period. The rail had, of course, been built to better integrate Kenya into the international capitalist order. But, surely, independent Kenya could have built more rails, more roads, more infrastructure to enable greater mobility of goods and services within Kenya, to secure the economic integrity of the country by, first, meeting its own needs and, only then, exporting the surplus in fair exchange. But foreign Western interests became as paramount in the post-Independence Kenya as they were in the colonial days. Even under national flags, Africa's resources like copper, gold, diamonds, uranium and oil continued to be a curse rather than a blessing, except for that section of the middle class which received its share for its supervisory role. Is there any reason other than this cosy relationship to imperialist bourgeoisie that would make an oil-producing region suffer from broken roads, broken schools, broken hospitals, broken houses for the many while a few wallow in luxuries and indulge in shopping sprees to Western capitals? No reinvestment in the region, in the country, in the people?

Even more negative is the political fallout, with the consciousness that had risen to visions of national unity, African unity and pan-Africanism now become regionalized and eventually vulgarized into myopic ethnic and clan horizons. The one-party state with the supreme leader is born, and, of course, the inevitable military dictatorships tolerated (and in some cases initiated) by the West in the era of the Cold War. The widest vision beyond the supreme leader's self-aggrandizement is the ethnic. But it is not ethnic in the sense of a community wallowing in luxury but, rather, in the sense of a vulgar elite touting its vulgarity and myopia as the vision of the entire ethnicity, fighting with the other equally vulgar elite of another ethnicity for crumbs from the imperialist table. The leader, while wearing the colours of the national flag, surrounds himself with cronies and sycophants, be they from his village or other regions. His reception by Western leaders, with the inevitable patting on the back for being a faithful ally, becomes its own reward. The military vote and the armed nod from the West—and not the people—are all he needs to maintain power. And yet, when the same elite is cornered and asked to account for its crimes against its own people, it has no problem in shamelessly resurrecting the anti-imperialist slogans of yesterday.

The fact is, when it comes to turning his back on the people, the leader—be he a military or civilian dictator —is representative of the middle class[10] which, partially or wholly, is quickly able to forget that its power is located among the people. Sometimes, it is not even aware of its total identification with the outlook of its Western counterparts. This is because the middle class' memory of being has become so completely integrated with that of the European bourgeoisie that such oblivion seems normal and natural. The European capitals of the former colonial powers (London, Paris, Amsterdam, Brussels, Lisbon, Rome) have become the social mecca for sections of this class—their shopping neighbour-hoods and the Swiss banks the safe locations of the loot from the nation.

The economic and political praxis of the ruling mid-dle class that systematically excludes the majority are rooted in the culture it has uncritically absorbed. Its heroes are often the strongmen of the imperialist era: Napoleon, in the case of Jean-Bédel Bokassa, who moulded his self-crowning as emperor of Central African Republic on that of his hero; Winston Churchill, whose belligerent sayings in defence of the British empire are often on the lips of some politicians. Many behave as if they have a God-given right to rule on the basis of their ethnicity. The word governor, with all its colonial and anti-democratic ring, has become the most beloved title for newly created figures of regional power.

It is not hard to see the roots of this identification with cultural symbols of Western power. The education of the black elite is entirely in European languages. Their conceptualization of the world is within the parameters of the language of their inheritance. Most importantly, it makes the elite an integral part of a global-speech community. Within the African nations, European tongues continue to be what they were during the colonial period: the languages of power, conception and articulation of the worlds of science, technology, politics, law, commerce, administration and even culture. Most African nations are thereby divided into two: a tiny group within the privileged linguistic loop, but which cuts across the various ethnic boundaries; and the majority, speaking different ethnic languages but united by their location outside the linguistic loop in every possible way. Fanon touches on this problem in *Black Skin, White Masks* (1952) when he claims that to acquire a colonial language is to acquire the weight of the civilization it carries, including its concepts of how reality is organized. The tiny group that speaks it is drawn from the top 5 per cent in each of the ethnic nationalities but it may come to see itself as somehow constituting the nation. By cutting across the various ethnicities, the language of power may seem to be the more national. The middle class' incorporation into European memory,[11] before and after Independence, is a major weakness of the class, a point Fanon emphasizes when he accuses the national bourgeoisie of identifying with the Western bourgeoisie from whom 'it has learnt by heart' its lessons.[12]

III

The linguistic incorporation of the African elite into the European memory[13] has dire consequences for Africa, the most obvious being the almost universal acceptance by African states and educated Africans that English, French and Portuguese are the proper languages for producing and storing knowledge and information. This has meant that the masses, the social agency of change, are being denied access to the knowledge and information they most need to change the world. Trickle-down economics, so beloved of capitalist fundamentalists, is reflected in trickle-down education, information and knowledge. I have talked a great deal about this problem in my books *Decolonizing the Mind* (1986) and *Penpoints, Gunpoints and Dreams* (1998), and the more I consider the situation, the more I feel that the linguistic incorporation of the African educated elite

into the European bourgeois memory is an active con-
tributor to Africa's backwardness. In that sense, every
educated African who remains doggedly locked within
the linguistic walls of European languages, irrespective
of his avowed social vision (of the Right or Left), is part
of the problem and not the solution. European memory
sits like a dead weight on the self-imagination of Africa
and it prevents the elite, even the most radical of them,
from connecting itself to what Fanon describes as the revolutionary capital[14]—which is the people. The revolutionary leafleteering that flooded the Kenyan streets
during the years of struggle against the Moi dictatorship
were nearly all in English. Unlike the leaflets against the
colonial dictatorship, which were always in African languages and hence impacted the struggle by helping people understand colonialism and be better able to fight it,
the leaflets against postcolonial misrule hardly add anything to the popular imagination because of the languages
in which they are written. More than anything else, it is
this incorporation that prevents Africans from thinking
of alternatives outside the Western hegemonic economic-
political-cultural matrix.

The ruling elite, for instance, still clings to Europe's
conceptualization of the nation-state. In precapitalist times,
the world was largely without protected borders which
were a crime to cross. Borders were often the point of
mutual exchange and, in some cases, the site of intellectual
and cultural cross-currents. Borders united more than they

divided. The nation-state, the form in which capitalist modernity organized its power, was born with notions of ownership in general and of territory in particular. The European nation-state, the slave plantation, the colony and the prison are simultaneous products of the same moment in history.

It is not surprising that these institutions have similar features. The primary one is that of an enclosed space, often with a single point of entry and exit. They are gated spaces with a supervising authority. Like all such spaces, the gate is guarded all the time. One cannot enter or exit without the approval of the all-seeing centralized authority and surveillance system. The comings and goings are recorded meticulously. The border now becomes a wall, separating those within from those without.

The plantation, the colony, the prison and the nation-state mimic and anticipate one another in more ways. The slave plantation is implicated with the eighteenth-century enclosure movement in England in which peasants were hounded out of common lands to become reservoirs of labour in congested towns.[15] Those who turned to stealing sheep as a means of livelihood were hanged. But later they were exported to colonies-as-prisons. A good number of colonies, including Australia and Angola, doubled as settlements and penal territories. It is not surprising, for instance, that in France, the minister for prisons was also in charge of colonies.[16] The nation-state is built on division, separation and central control, with the prison playing an increasingly significant role in its exercise of power.

Today, some countries have prison populations that could constitute a separate nation. The surveillance system of the prison—the Orwellian state of *1984*—is taken as an unquestionable norm of the everyday. Big Brother watches even from outer space but is otherwise most visibly present at airports, the streets, and even, at times, inside homes.

The European nation-state created what Aimé Césaire, in his *Discourse on Colonialism* (1955), sees as the intractable problem of the proletariat within its borders and of the colony outside its borders. The colonial state itself was a creation of the European nation-state. Remaining subject to the mother country, the colonial, as such, was not an independent entity in international relations. It acted more like a military force of occupation on behalf of the mother state. But in form, it was a mimicry of the European nation-state and was constructed on the contradictory practices of enclosure (the plantation), integration and separation.

The most significant division of Africa was into spheres of influence and control by the European powers that met in Berlin in 1884. The divisions and boundaries were most arbitrary, often combining different nations into one geographic entity while dividing other nations into splinter entities under different powers. The Somali nation is the best example of a people who shared a territory,

language, culture, and history being split five ways—into
French Djibouti, Italian Somaliland, British Somaliland,
British Kenya and feudal Ethiopia. The story is the same
throughout the continent. Colonial boundaries were both
arbitrary and divisive. Within the colony, the colonial
state dispossessed the former land-owning, independent
and communal farmers whom, in historical imitation of
the English enclosure movement, it hounded into towns
to create a reservoir of labour. The colonial state survived
challenge after challenge from the dispossessed and the
new proletariat by ensuring that the communities within
its territorial boundary remained divided on ethnic and
religious lines. Thus, for instance, in Kenya, between 1922
and 1960, up to two years before Independence, Africans
were not allowed to form political unions that encom-
passed the territory as a whole. The colonial state also
thrived on the co-optation of a nascent middle class into
an alliance of convenience. The army, the police and the
prisons worked together to maintain the colonial state
against a restive population; otherwise why would
Kenya, Uganda and Tanzania (all British colonial states)
need to have different territorial armies? The same is true
for the former Nyasaland, now Malawi, and the two
British Rhodesias, now Zambia and Zimbabwe! The
postcolonial African independent state was simply a
nationalization of the colonial state, with the inherited
territorial boundaries now sanctified by necessity and,
more significantly, by the inability of the new classes in
power to imagine a different form of the state. Among all

the emergent postcolonial leaders, it was only Nkrumah and Nyerere who talked of their nation-states as partially sovereign and were willing to forgo the status of a sovereign being for a union with other African states. Otherwise, African identities as nations were mapped, marked and named for Africa by the former colonial overlords, and the African middle class was wedded to maintaining the same borders where they did not actually call for their curvature into clan and village kingdoms.

Yet Africans need only take a cursory glance at their history to see that the most successful moments in their struggles were those that challenged the way they were defined and grouped by European colonizing memory. Pan-Africanism is the best example. Initially imagined by diasporic African intellectuals and nourished by additional ideas from continental Africans, this vision was a creative response to European divisions of Africa. 'Africa for the Africans at home and abroad,' cried Garvey. Edward Wilmot Blyden, H. Silvester Williams, Amy Ashwood Garvey, W. E. B. Du Bois, C. L. R. James, Kwame Nkrumah, George Padmore, Frantz Fanon and a whole range of others—men and women—imagined a united Africa that would be the base for all peoples of African descent. They envisioned an Africa without internal borders, an Africa playing its legitimate role in the community of nations. The pinnacle of this vision was the Fifth Pan-African Congress in Manchester, England, in 1945, a conference that resulted in the return to Africa of leaders like Nkrumah and Kenyatta with renewed vigour and energy. *Africa Must Unite* (1963), penned by Nkrumah, declared that the Independence of Ghana in 1957 was meaningless without the liberation of the entire continent. Europe laughed at him, even mocked him. But look at the reversal of the situation. The Europeans that used to decry calls for pan-Africanist unity and an African Union government are the ones who are now uniting as the European Union, with a common parliament, a common currency and freedom of movement across the borders. A united Europe will obviously be in a stronger position to obtain a better share of the resources of a globalized world. But Africa, sold on the outmoded European concept of the nation-state, has retreated from the pan-African vision which got the continent the few gains it still holds on to; it has retreated into national borders and even further, into ethnic and clan states which will have to negotiate with the increasing power of European and American blocs from a position of increasing weakness.

It is clear that if Africa is to make progress, the African elite must return to its real base: *the people*. An authentic middle class in an underdeveloped country, wrote Fanon, should repudiate its colonially fated role as the tool of capitalism, 'and to become entirely subservient to the revolutionary capital the people represent'. Such a class, he continues, ought to 'make available to them the intellectual and technical capital it culled from its time in colonial universities'.[17] This repudiation would mean nothing less than the intellectual faction of the middle class, the African intelligentsia, disentangling itself from the European memory by rejecting the notion that European languages are the only legitimate means of organizing and articulating reality and dreams. They should not become prisoners of their very success at snatching knowledge in universities at home and abroad. The retrieval and use of the languages of the people is of paramount importance. A return to the base, the people, must mean at the very least the use of a language and languages that the people speak. Any further linguistic additions should be for strengthening, deepening and widening this power of the languages spoken by the people.

Is it not a blot on the self-esteem of a whole continent that up until now, outside Ethiopia, not a single treaty exists between Africa and the rest of the world in an African language? Instead of challenging this situation, the African intelligentsia as a whole has surrendered, without even an attempt at resistance, before what it sees as an insurmountable hurdle It 'disappears with its soul set at peace'[18] into the comfort zone of European languages. The dreams of Africa remain swaddled in European sounds, inaccessible to African people. The abandonment of the people by its intellectuals, for whom the people have endured hardships in order to get them educated—with the expectation of fruitful returns—is the real triumph of colonialism and a dishonour to the broader African intelligentsia.

Fortunately, there have always been a few intellectuals who have refused to abdicate and have kept the issue alive. In Ethiopia, there has always been intellectual work produced in African languages. The nineteenth- and early-twentieth-century Xhosa and Zulu intellectuals debated the best language of African modernity, with some, such as Samuel Mqayi and Benedict Wallet Vilakazi, standing firmly for African languages. This advocacy is continued in the work of Cheikh Anta Diop and Obi Wali. Currently, there are signs that African intellectuals are beginning to think seriously about the call for African languages, as expressed, for example, in the work of Kwesi Kwaa Prah. The Centre for African Studies, based in Cape Town, has become an important advocate for the centrality of African languages in the realm of education, technology and science. Some governments, notably those of South Africa and Eritrea, have tried to come up with enlightened policies on African languages. In many ways, the conference on literature and knowledge in African languages, held in Eritrea at the beginning of 2000, was a turning point. The conference came up with the Asmara Declaration which called on African languages to take on the duty, the responsibility and the challenge of speaking for the continent. This was really a call for Africa to reconnect with its memory and to engage with the world from its base. The 10 points[19] are a manifesto of the only means by which the African intelligentsia can heed Fanon's call to place its intellectual production at the people's disposal and hence connect itself with the revolutionary capital—the people. This is a fundamental step in Africa's search for a way out of the global quagmire: to arm our people with the knowledge and information that make them better equipped to effectively demand their rightful share of the globe.

It is also clear that Africa has to heed, as a matter of urgency, Nkrumah's call that 'Africa Must Unite'. Africa cannot be split into tiny political and economic units and command its share of the globe. But aren't the two proposals a contradiction? Can an Africa of many languages and cultural tendencies unite?

The perception of an irresolvable contradiction persists because of the assumption that monolingualism is the *sine qua non* of modernity. This also leads to the historical fiction of other societies being marked by monoculturalism. If we think broadly and historically, then we can see that this is not really the case. Even Europe has many languages (100 at least). And if we count the ones brought in by recent immigrants, then we are talking of hundreds of languages and autonomous dialects. The US, with its 50 states, has more languages, religions and ethnicities than any other territorial nation-state in the world. The official posture may be that of a linguistic melting pot but the reality on the ground speaks otherwise. In Canada, the language question continues. The existence of many languages is not a particularly African problem. On the face of it, it is not a problem at all. Still, the assumption persists that many languages are incompatible with unity and a continental African identity. It was this that made Diop, in 1948, respond to 'the objection, usually raised, that Africans can never have linguistic unity', with the dismissive rejoinder that 'it is absolutely false to think that this apparent multiplicity of languages is a serious impediment to the establishment of an indigenous culture', arguing that the 600 languages could be merged into four major languages, 'capable of being developed [into] instruments for the expression of the entire African thought. And this only requires will power, firmness and determination on the part of Africans to liberate themselves intellectually and morally.'[20]

It is not necessary to argue for four main languages in order to make the point that the multiplicity of languages is not a barrier to development. Africans have to admit that in each country there are many nationalities and languages, and accept that reality as the starting point. This brings us to the question: How can the languages be used to bring about the unity of African peoples within a country and within the continent?

Enriching the languages people use and encouraging dialogue among them through the tool of translation is the best way to create a cultural basis for African unity. Imagine if all the books written in different African languages, and even those produced by continental and diasporic Africans in any language, were available in each and every African language. Would this not create a sense of common inheritance and a basis for more intellectual production? If an inter-ethnic, inter-regional continental language should emerge (hopefully not on the graveyard of other languages), that would be a gain for Africa and add another dimension to the conversation among African languages.

Paramount is the rejection of the outlook that a united Africa is a union of African heads of state; it has to be replaced by the notion and practice of a union of the African peoples. The struggle and the process to regain control of human and natural resources are not the sole business of heads of state but of all the African peoples, with their varied languages and cultures.

If Africans put people first, they would clearly see the damage done by colonial boundaries that perpetuate European memory as the basis for their definition of national being. Driven by this 'people awareness', Africa should look at the colonial borders and ask different questions. In so doing, it can turn what is seemingly a weakness into strength. Africa can turn the division of peoples of the same language and culture, but who span different borders, into its strength by viewing those peoples as a shared community.

In nearly each African state, there are people of the same language, culture and history on either side of the border—these are called border communities. For instance, if Kenya, Ethiopia, Djibouti and Somalia themselves were to see the Somali people as a shared community, then a union of these countries would not be a union of cultural strangers. The notion and values of a shared community become links in a chain for African unity from the Cape to Cairo, from Somalia to Liberia. A good number of border communities have a common spiritual leader and, in reality, they do not recognize the colonial boundaries that divide them. In their cultural practices, they are challenging the sanctity of the colonially derived nation-state. Again, should Africa not use these communities, with their common spiritual authority and history, to unite, instead of criminalizing their border crossings? In short, Africa should truly imagine an internally borderless continent, except for purposes of administration of production and distribution of services. The guiding vision should be to turn the borders into highways for the movement of goods, services and ideas across the continent. Then will come to fruition the visions of the forbearers who saw the continent as a material and spiritual abode for Africans at home and abroad.

IV

A borderless Africa, or, rather, one where the national states have mutated into a continental federal state, cannot be brought about by force.

The process of its becoming, in fact, assumes that democracy, in the Lincolnian sense of the rule, is the driving force. The alternative is raw force, which would not bring about political integration but, rather, disintegration through border wars. Continental unity, for it to be real, must be voluntary and people-driven.

Africa must, however, not confuse the Lincolnian definition of democracy with that currently practised in the West, the US in particular, where it has been turned into a billionaire democracy, billiocracy or dollarcracy. Such a democracy in the West has become a four- or five-year moneyocratic ritual. A people-driven democracy should be about the society people want to build and not about people holding elections every four years or so to choose among moneyocrats. Elections are important, of course, but they should be part of the overall search for a just society.

In this sense, there has always been a major flaw in the Western democratic tradition, from ancient Athens to present-day US. The Athenian democracy was based on the division of society into free men, women and slaves. Democracy was for the free citizen. Democracy as exercised by colonial powers assumed freedom at home and colonial slavery abroad. It is still the case. The dominant powers go to great lengths, including deception, to ensure that their population is compliant in the policies they want to carry out at home and abroad. Yet they become impatient with foreign governments that refuse to circumvent the wishes of their people and thereby decline to do the bidding of the West.

The neocolonial framework cannot be the foundation or even the cornerstone of African unity. Only a consistent anti-neocolonialism and a people-driven democracy can form such a foundation. In fact, such a people-driven democracy may be at odds with representative democracy, which often means that the people are passive viewers as their representatives in parliament exercise power on their behalf. Democracy must mean daily accountability and not four-yearly counting of coins necessary to buy the vote.

In the exercise of democracy, Africa may once again want to learn a few lessons from its precolonial institutions. The two dominant types of societies in Africa, the one without a centralized authority and the other with a centralized authority vested in the chief, both assumed forms of participatory democracy. Kenyatta, in his book *Facing Mount Kenya* (1938), describes such a participatory process among the Agikuyu of Kenya. What is striking in the picture he draws is the practice of self-organization at all levels of society. Even young people had their own councils and thus learnt leadership as part of their everyday life. This is in stark contrast to the practices of the colonial and postcolonial state that see organized people as enemies of the state. How many times have we seen youth organizations banned, with police chasing them down the streets of major cities and towns? A

combination of participatory and representative democratic practices may well be what Africa needs as the
means of realizing and exercising the dreams of a creative
African unity.

But even before a political union, Africa has to start
the process of economic and communications integration
and create an all-Africa common market. The models are
already there, the best being the East African Community, which once saw Kenya, Uganda and Tanzania share
a host of services, including a common currency (before
a colonized nation-statism gleefully broke it). But such a
common market can only endure if it rises to the level of
a political union. A continental political union will speed
up economic integration. An economically and politically
united Africa will also be in a better position to engage
the other forces in the world in the struggle for a more
just global community. Whatever the path towards a
continental identity, it calls for a serious questioning and
rejection of the sanctity of colonial boundaries.

This is nothing short of a call for the decolonization
of the economies, politics and cultures of Africa, in order
to create a new beginning for Africa. Even this will not
be smooth sailing. The forces of global reaction will still
try to divide and dominate. But Africa has to meet this
reaction with proaction for the sake of its own being in a
rapidly globalizing world.

Some cynics, schooled in crippling self-doubt, will see
in such a call a dream of the impossible. But dreams have

always drawn images of the ideally possible. In imagination, we draw outlines of a future, then try to realize it. In the days when a few humans began conceiving of flying, they were dubbed dreamers, not realists. But they continued dreaming and trying. During plantation slavery, those who talked of freedom were seen as dreamers. But they did not stop dreaming and trying to realize it. It is the same for dreamers of the anticolonial resistance, who continued to imagine victory and work towards it. Our present-day world owes a lot to those who dared to dream.

For a long time now, I have advocated moving the centre from a handful of European nations to marginalized nations,[21] and then creating conditions for a healthy dialogue and equal exchange among them all. Although this has been couched in mainly linguistic and cultural terms, my concerns embrace the wholeness of a community—the economic, political, cultural and psychic. This wholeness can never be any but that which is rooted in the people—not the middle class masquerading as 'we the people', literally substituting itself for the people. I see all these as the interrelated complexity we call human societies, as opposed to the current forms of globalization that often mean the appropriation of all the other centres and their resources to serve one 'supercentre'.

In short, there should be a distinction between globalization and globalism—the one being the process of making the world borderless for finance capital; the other, that of making it borderless for the people. The visible success of globalization is a glossy middle class; that of globalism is prosperous creative people, their common humanity expressed in the multicoloured particularities.

For an Africa ready to find its place in the world, the best advice is still the one given by Fanon in the conclusion to *The Wretched of the Earth*, where he rejects the European model because in its history, technology and progress, he sees an avalanche of murders, a succession of negations of the human. He urges the forces of progressive change to not pay tribute to Europe by creating states, institutions and societies which draw their inspiration from it, concluding that if Africa wants to become a new Europe, 'then let us leave the destiny of our countries to Europeans. They will know how to do it better than the most gifted among us.' He is very clear in his call for the more creative path to follow—and it's not one of mindless mimicry: 'Let us decide not to imitate Europe; let us combine our muscles and our brains in a new direction. Let us try to create the whole man (and woman), whom Europe has been incapable of bringing to triumphant birth.'[22]

Current Europe and the rest of the West are not an ideal to aspire for but a failure of vision from which to learn a lesson. Hopefully, the lesson is one that will intensify the ongoing people-based social struggles and lead to a grand alliance of global people power. Africa will then find its true identity in contributing and drawing equally from a common global human endeavour.

Notes

1 Robert C. Tucker (ed.), *The Marx–Engels Reader*, 2ND EDN (New York: W. W. Norton, 1978), pp. 476–7.

2 Ibid., p. 474.

3 GATT mutated into the World Trade Organization in 1994.

4 For Margaret Thatcher's 'There Is No Alternative', see James H. Mittleman, 'Alternative Globalization' in Richard Sandbrook (ed.), *Civilizing Globalization* (New York: State University of New York Press, 2003), pp. 237–52; here, p, 237.

5 The US and Canada, for instance, heavily subsidize their agricultural and steel sectors but seethe in fury and demand that the WTO pass judgement on others that follow suit.

6 It could be said that the only true NGOs are those in the postcolonial state, because those in the West are often subdivisions of the foreign policies of their governments.

7 Note the celebrated meeting between US president Ronald Reagan and the Afghan mujahidin on 21 March 1983 at the Oval Office, during which he called them

'freedom fighters'. Available at: http://www.reagan.-utexas.edu/archives/speeches/1983/32183e.htm (last accessed on 27 March 2015).

8   For data, see Kwame Nkrumah, *Neo-colonialism: The Last Stage of Imperialism* (London: Nelson, 1965).

9   Frantz Fanon, *The Wretched of the Earth* (Richard Philcox trans.) (New York: Grove Press, 2004), p. 100.

10 Chinua Achebe's novel *Anthills of the Savannah* (1988) dramatizes what is true of the postcolonial situation in Africa as a whole: the fact that the military man and his intellectual collaborators as well as opponents are often products of the same schools and colleges.

11 See my book *Something Torn and New: An African Renaissance* (New York: BasicCivitas Books, 2009) in which I talk about the politics of memory.

12 Fanon, *Wretched of the Earth*, p. 119.

13 For more of this, see again Ngũgĩ, *Something Torn and New*.

14 Fanon, *Wretched of the Earth*, p. 99.

15 See Karl Polanyi's discussion of the enclosure movement in *The Great Transformation* (Boston, MA: Beacon Press, 1944).

16 See Michel Foucault, *Discipline and Punish: The Birth of the Prison* (Alan Sheridan trans.) (New York: Vintage Books, 1995).

17 Fanon, *Wretched of the Earth*, p. 99.

18 Ibid. Fanon is talking about the retreat of the middle class as a whole into what he describes as 'the shocking ways [. . .] of a traditional bourgeoisie'.

19 (i) African languages must take on the duty, the responsibility and the challenge of speaking for the continent.

(ii) The vitality and equality of African languages must be recognized as a basis for the future empowerment of African peoples. (iii) The diversity of African languages reflects the rich cultural heritage of Africa and must be used as an instrument of African unity. (iv) Dialogue among African languages is essential: African languages must use the instrument of translation to advance communication among all people, including the disabled. (v) All African children have the inalienable right to attend school and learn in their mother tongues. Every effort should be made to develop African languages at all levels of education. (vi) Promoting research on African languages is vital for their development, while the advancement of African research and documentation will be best served by the use of African languages. (vii) The effective and rapid development of science and technology in Africa depends on the use of African languages and modern technology must be used for the development of African languages. (viii) Democracy is essential for the equal development of African languages, and African languages are vital for the development of democracy based on equality and social justice. (ix) African languages, like all languages, contain gender bias. The role of African languages in development must overcome this gender bias and achieve gender equality. (x) African languages are essential for the decolonization of African minds and for the African Renaissance.

20 Cheikh Anta Diop, 'When Can We Talk of an African Renaissance', *Le Musée* (November 1948); reprinted in *Towards the African Renaissance: Essays in African Culture and Development, 1946–1960* (Egbuna P. Modum trans.) (London: Karnak House, 1996), p. 37.

21 See my book *Moving the Center*: *The Struggle for Cultural Freedoms* (Oxford: James Currey / Nairobi: East African Educational Publishers, 1993).

22 Fanon, *Wretched of the Earth*, p. 236.

NEW FRONTIERS OF KNOWLEDGE

The Challenge of the
Pan-Africanist Social Scientist

In 1978, locked up in a maximum-security prison in Kenya for a work I had done in an African language, I wrote defiantly to my jailers, asserting that African intellectuals must do for their languages and cultures what all other intellectuals in history have done for theirs. This is still the challenge of our history as African social scientists and scholars.

Despite her vast natural and human resources, indeed, despite the fact that Africa has always provided, albeit unwillingly, resources that have fuelled capitalist modernity to its current stage of globalization, Africa gets the rawest deal. This is obvious in the areas of economic and political power. But this is also reflected in the production and consumption of information and knowledge.

As in the political and economic fields, Africa has been a player in the production of knowledge. The increase in the number of universities and research centres, though with often shrinking resources, have shaped great African producers of knowledge in all fields, such that brilliant sons and daughters of Africa are to be found in all the universities in the world. The constellation of thinkers and researchers around CODESRIA is a testament to this. So why the raw deal for Africa, even in the consumption of knowledge produced by her sons and daughters?

The founders of CODESRIA in 1973 were driven by the noble aim of developing scientific capacities and tools that would further the cohesion, well-being and development of African societies. These founding visionaries were very clear that the council would be considered meaningful only if a conscious effort was made to foster a pan-African community of intellectual workers active in and connected to the continent, the accent being on commitment to that connection.

But are African intellectuals and their production really connected to the continent? Even from a cursory glance at the situation, it is clear that there is a discrepancy between the quality and quantity of production of knowledge exemplified by CODESRIA and the quality and quantity of its consumption by the general populace. Ours has been a case of trickle-down knowledge, a variation of the theory of trickle-down economics, a character of capitalist modernity, reflected more particularly in its colonial manifestation.

Since our very mandate as African producers of knowledge is to connect with the continent, it behooves us to continually re-examine our entire colonial heritage, which includes the theory and practice of trickle-down knowledge. This means, in effect, our having to continually examine our relationship to European memory in the organization of knowledge.

In my book *Something Torn and New*, I have written extensively and intensively about how Europe planted its memory on Africa's landscape (or wherever in the world it went) mapping, surveying the land and then naming it as a claim of discovery and ownership. The planting was extended to the African body: Western Christianity became a vast renaming ritual reminiscent of that horror scene in Sembene Ousmane's film *Ceddo* (1977) where this ownership and identity is branded on the body of the enslaved with a hot iron. The body becomes a book, a parchment, where ownership and identity are forever inscribed.

But the biggest branding was that of the intellect through language. Language is a means of organizing and conceptualizing reality; it is also a bank for the memory generated by human interaction with the natural and social environment. Each language, no matter how small, carries its memory of the world. Suppressing and degrading the languages of the colonized meant also marginalizing the memory they carried and elevating to universality the memory carried by the language of the conqueror. This obviously includes elevation of that language's conceptualization of the world, including that of self and others.

In the relationship between Prospero and Caliban in Shakespeare's *Tempest* (1616), we get illuminations of colonial knowledge and scholarship and, in fact, its very method. Initially, it is the native informant who knows everything about the immediate environment, including the location of water and means of survival. It is the native informant who imparts this local knowledge to the colonial intellectual, in the form of an explorer or administrator who recodes it in his language. Historically, we get the same process in the encounter between Christopher Columbus and the Amerindian world he thinks is Asia. Columbus' journal is among the earliest of a long line of other intellectual servants of capitalist modernity renaming the landscape. After waxing rhapsodic about the beauty of the Caribbean islands and the generous reception by the natives, Columbus then seizes some of them 'in order that they might learn and give me information of that which there is in these parts . . . I shall take them with me.'[1] Learning, or shall we say education, is tied in with capture and enslavement. Presumably, what he learns from the learned captives is coded in Columbus' European language—in this case, Portuguese—and it becomes the primary source for future scholars and researchers, the original utterances having been lost in translation. This pattern, of the outsider looking in, continues into modern scholarship where, helped by a native informant, or research assistant, the scholar records statements, translated to him in, say English, and these notes become the primary data, the original text in the original language lost for ever. What the outsider now says of place, his memory of place, becomes the primary source of subsequent additions to knowledge of place.

I want to suggest that our various fields of knowledge of Africa are in many ways rooted in that colonial tradition of the outsider looking in, gathering knowledge with the help of native informants, and then storing the final product in a European language for consumption by those who have access to that language. Anthropology, the study of the insider by the outsider, for the consumption of those who share the culture of the anthropologist, permeates the genealogy of European studies of Africa. We, the inheritors and bearers of that tradition, in many ways 'anthropologize' Africa, especially in method. We collect intellectual items and put them in European-language museums and archives. Africa's global visibility through European languages has meant Africa's invisibility in African languages. Our knowledge of Africa is largely filtered through European languages and their vocabulary.

There are those, of course, who will argue that African languages are incapable of handling complexities of social thought, or that they do not have adequate vocabularies for accommodating the concepts of Western rationality. This objection was answered long ago by one of the brightest intellects from Africa, Cheikh Anita Diop, when he argued that no language had a monopoly of cognitive vocabulary, that every language could develop its terms for science and technology. This is the position being maintained by contemporary thinkers like Kwesi Kwaa Prah whose Centre for Advanced Studies of African Society (CASAS), based in Cape Town, South Africa, of which he is director, is doing so much to advocate the use of African languages in all fields of learning, including scientific thought. Other places with similar advocacy include that of the philosopher Paulin Hountondji, at the African Centre for Advanced Studies, based in Porto-Novo, Benin, which intends to promote African languages as media for African scientific thought.

There have been other individuals, such as the late Neville Alexander of Cape Town, who chaired the committee that came up with the very enlightened South African policy on languages, and Kwesi Wiredu, who long ago called on African philosophers to engage issues in African languages. This advocacy has a long history going back to the Xhosa intellectuals of the late nineteenth century and continued among Zulu intellectuals of the 1940s.

All these intellectuals have tried to debunk the claims of an inadequacy of words and terms for abstract or scientific thought in African languages. In practice, the continued Ethiopian scholarship in African languages belies the negative claims, and it should not be forgotten that even early modern English and French had to overcome similar claims of inadequacy as vehicles for philosophy and scientific thought against the then dominant Latin. Those languages needed the courage of their intellectuals to break out of the dominance of Latin memory. In the introduction to his *Discourse on Method* (1637), René Descartes defends his use of vernacular for philosophic thought against similar claims of inadequacy of French.

What African languages need is a similar commitment from African intellectuals. It only needs courage and hard work, as exemplified by the case of Dr Gatua wa Mbugua. In May 2003, a graduate student at Cornell University, Mbugua presented and successfully defended his master's thesis on bio-intensive agriculture, written in the Gĩkũyũ language, to the Department of Crop Science. For Mbugua, it meant sheer dedication and lots of work, for he had to provide an English translation of his thesis: 'The Impact of Bio-intensive Cropping on Yields and Nutrient Contents of Collared Greens in Kenya'. Later, Mbugwa joined the University of Wyoming, where he did research in the central highlands of the area, recording his data in Gĩkũyũ. He later successfully defended his PhD dissertation, which he also wrote in Gĩkũyũ, before auto-translating it for the purposes of his teachers who, of course, had to evaluate the scientific content and did not know Gĩkũyũ. As far as I know, Mbũgwa's work is the first scientific work in Gĩkũyũ at any university in or outside Africa. He had no tradition on which to fall back, not even that of a stable scientific vocabulary, but this did not daunt his spirits.

There are cynics who will respond to this with: So what? The Gĩkũyũ language cannot sustain a written

intellectual production. The Gĩkũyũ people number
about 6 million; the Danes about 5 million. All the books
written and published in Gĩkũyũ cannot fill up a shelf;
books written and published in Danish number thousands
and exhaust the shelves of many libraries. The Yoruba
people number nearly 40 million; the Swedes about 9 million. But intellectual production in the two languages is
vastly different. Why is it that 40 million Africans cannot
sustain such production whereas 9 million Swedes can?
Icelanders, who number about 300,000, have one of the
most flourishing intellectual productions in Europe.
What a little over a quarter of a million Icelanders can,
surely 6 million Gĩkũyũ are also capable of. We talk of
Greek and Latin intellectual heritage and forget that it
originated in city-states. The vaunted Italian Renaissance
and its rich and varied heritage in the arts, architecture
and learning were largely from the different regions of
Italy—Rome, Florence, Mantua, Venice and Genoa.
What the vernaculars of these small city-states, princi-
palities and regions achieved by way of intellectual production can be achieved by any other similarly situated
languages.

The question remains: What would be the place of
European languages in scholarship? It is only because we
all had to learn them that we use them—there is nothing
inherently global and universal about them; they just
happen to be the languages of power. However, no matter
how we may think of the historical process by which they
came to occupy the place they now do in our lives, it is a

fact that English and French have enabled international visibility of the African presence. But they have achieved this by uprooting the intellectuals from their linguistic and cultural bases. They have merely invited African intellectuals to operate within European memory. European languages also have the immense deposits of some of the best in literary and general African thought. They are granaries of African intellectual productions, and these productions as a whole are the nearest thing to a common pan-African social property. This, in fact, defines best the mission we should assign to French and English: use these European languages to enable dialogue among African languages and their visibility in the community of world languages, instead of as a tool to disable them by uprooting intellectuals and their production from their original language base. In short, use English and French to enable and not to disable.

This then is the challenge of social science in Africa today: How best to connect with the African continent in the era of globalization? How do we create and strengthen a common African base from which to engage with the world? African economic, political and cultural unity is surely the answer. While political unity and economic integration lie in the realm of decisions taken by political leadership, African intellectuals are bound by their very calling to create a common intellectual basis for that unity. There is need for a strong body of public intellectuals rooted in the common languages of the people to argue out, rationalize, popularize and make common the case for a genuine people-based African union.

We cannot afford to be intellectual outsiders in our own land. We must reconnect with the buried alluvium of African memory—that must become the base for planting African memory anew in the continent and in the world. This can only result in the empowerment of African languages and cultures and make them pillars of a more self-confident Africa ready to engage with the world, through give-and-take, from its base in African memory.

Note

1 Quoted in Bronwyn Mills, 'Caribbean Cartographies: Maps, Cosmograms, and the Caribbean Imagination', unpublished PhD dissertation, Department of Comparative Literature, New York University, New York, 2004, n.p.

SPLENDOUR IN SQUALOR

*The Global Responsibility
to Protect Humanity*

The phrase 'responsibility to protect' brings to my mind painful memories of the lack of protection of many who died in ethnic clashes in Kenya in 2007, following disputed presidential elections. The character of the gruesome scenes was captured in the story of a child fleeing from the flames of a torched church where he and his parents had sought refuge only to be captured and thrown back into the flames. In pre-colonial times, even times of war among neighbouring communities, there had always been rules protecting children and women. Questions asked by survivors expressed shock and incomprehension: They were our neighbours; our children played together; how could they do this to us?

The scene was set for counter-acts of ethnic cleansing, the new wave of victims connected to the original perpetrators by only their ethnicity. Ordinary working people, often united by their poverty, were set against one another by a middle-class political elite tele-guiding the horror from the safety of their city palaces and cocktail circuits. The state seemed unable to control the situation. It failed to act. It failed the nation.

Far away in California, I felt paralysed by helplessness, which must have been a thousand times more intense for those in the country. In response to a call from the BBC, I could think of the United Nations as the only body that could intervene, investigate and, hopefully, hold to account those who incited the war of poor on poor. As it turned out, it was the efforts of the United Nations, through Kofi Annan as emissary, that eventually helped in putting down the flames, stopping the flow of blood, and creating the space for an uneasy peace and, eventually, the mixed bag of a coalition government.

Even so, I knew that what was happening in my beloved Kenya had already been enacted in Rwanda, Bosnia, Iraq, and had precedence in the colonial and slave eras, reminding me of *Julius Caesar* (1599), where the assassins, after bathing in the blood of their victims, ask: 'How many ages hence / Shall this our lofty scene be acted ov'r, / In states unborn and accents yet unknown!'[1]

Yes, how many times! The very impressive report of the secretary general on the implementation of the responsibility to protect, derived from the thoughtful declaration of the 2005 World Summit, should be an excellent basis for a response to that question by Shakespeare. For, even one more time, anywhere in the world, is one time too many. It's time humanity was freed from the scourges of genocide, war crimes, ethnic cleansing and crimes against its very human essence.

The ideal calls for implementation. The devil, however, lies in the context of implementation in terms of definition, history and the contemporary global situation. Terms like 'international community' have often been too narrowly evoked to make it sound as if the West is the gatekeeper determining who is to be allowed into that community and who is to be outlawed, or, even more narrowly, that North America and Western Europe alone constitute the international community. The emphasis on the United Nations is the right one; but it should be noted that the United Nations, with the Security Council's blessings in particular, has sometimes been used as a cover to legitimize invasions and overthrow regimes that the West deems intolerable to its interests. In Africa, Patrice Lumumba of the Congo was brutally murdered with the eyes of the United Nations forces he had invited looking the other way.

Europe is disproportionately represented in the Security Council while one continent, Africa, has no veto at all. A degree of humility is called for in all nations, big and small, and a holier-than-thou attitude will not do, for the history of the modern tells of a more complicated story. The worst instances of genocide and wanton massacres of other people have come from Europe. Hitlerism was not an exception in the European history of relationship with other peoples. The generals who advised Hitler had honed their skills in the massacre and medical experimentation on the Herero people of Namibia. Every colonizing nation in the past has been involved in crimes against humanity. Slave trade and plantation slavery are obvious instances. Africa, America and Australia have stories of indigenous populations depleted, displaced by Europe.[2] In my own country, Kenya, in their war against the Mau Mau–led anticolonial movement, the British put thousands into concentration camps and villages almost as if they had taken to heart lessons from Hitler. It is not a matter of dwelling on the past. But the past has lessons for us all. The spectre of Rwanda will long haunt our memory and it is not any less a horror because the Belgian king Leopold II had wiped out and maimed a million others in the late nineteenth century, all for rubber and Belgian banks. Europe, with US backing, cannot be judge, jury and executioner. Many of the hot spots in the world today, more often than not, are consequences of a colonial history of divide, plunder and murder. The most monstrous dictators in Africa were products of the military academies of the Western world, schooled in a colonial practice predicated on the inhumanity of the colonized.

The United Nations document rightly calls for timely and decisive response. But working for and creating conditions that would make interventions unnecessary should be an integral part of the responsibility to protect. Rightly so, in the annexure, the document talks of early warning and assessment. But these should not be seen through subjective eyes. Subjectivity coloured by national and imperial interests may confuse prevention with pre-emption. Pre-emptive democracy is empty democracy. In fact, the subjective, coloured by self-interest, may prevent a clear sighting of those early warnings, one of which is right in front of our eyes—it is present in the economic world we have today.

There are two major fault lines in the world today. One is the division between a minority of very wealthy nations and a majority of very poor ones. The gap between them in terms of wealth and power increases and deepens daily. The irony is that this minority of nations consumes 90 per cent of the resources of the poor nations put together. When and where the resources of poor nations end up benefitting rich nations, the poor end up giving aid to the wealthy. This pattern is often reproduced within nations where some regions are wealthier, having become so by exploiting other regions in that territory. Oil may be discovered in one region but the benefits may bypass its dwellers. This is the vertical fault line between nations in the world and between regions in the same territory.

But within all nations (and even regions), there is another fault line—a horizontal one—between a minority of Haves and a majority of Have-Nots. The beggar and the homeless proliferate even in the major cities of the world. And yet, again, the minority of Haves depends on the majority of Have-Nots. The third figure, the prisoner, probably the fastest-growing demographic in all nations, is often hidden from view. Some nations have over a million people in prison, more than the population of quite a few United Nations member states. Thus, in the world today, there are imprisoned nations hidden behind the democratic facade of many countries. These two divisions of wealth and power, *between* nations and regions and *within* nations and regions, are the structural basis of the instability and of the many of the crimes we are talking about today.

I once visited the Cape Coast slave castle in Ghana. The architecture left a lasting impression on my mind. It had three levels. The top levels were the location of the governor's palace and the chapel. There were ample grounds for a ballroom and wedding-party receptions. But the ground levels of the same castle were the location of captive slaves waiting to be shipped across the Atlantic to America. The palace and the church were erected on the tombs of the enslaved. So while the enslaving wealthy were singing in gratitude to the Almighty and later moaning in the joy of bodily love in bed, the enslaved moaned in pain and groaned for deliverance. The cries of pleasure above contrasted with the cries of pain below, but the two were not unrelated. Splendour above was erected on the squalor below. The global palace today is built on a global prison. Splendour in squalor—there lies the basis of global instability.

So, if we are looking for long-term solutions that would make interventions unnecessary, we also ought to begin by questioning the view of development which focuses on the middle class and above. The middle class does not constitute a nation; people do, working people do. The development of a nation should then not be measured from the point of view of those at the top of the mountain but those at the bottom. Man-made poverty is also a crime against humanity. Even environmental crimes, committed largely by industrialized nations—the poisoning of waters, the corruption of the air we breathe, global warming, the production and proliferation of nuclear shit—are crimes against humanity.

Only by closing the two major divisions between nations/regions and within nations/regions can we begin to address the structural basis of crimes against humanity. That's why I think that the global community, through a strengthened and democratic United Nations and its organs, should look at structurally uneven development as an integral part of the responsibility to protect and implement. Pull down the grand global palace erected on global poverty and build the foundations of a new earth, a new world. End the global philosophy of splendour in squalor.

Notes

1　William Shakespeare, *Julius Caesar* in *Complete Works* (W. J. Craig ed.) (Oxford: Oxford University Press, 1943), 3.1.111–13, p. 832.

2　See, for example, David Stannard, *American Holocaust: The Conquest of the New World* (Oxford: Oxford University Press, 1992).

THE LEGACY OF SLAVERY

When, in my 2006 Harvard Lectures, I called for a month, a week—a day even—of collective mourning for the millions whose souls still cry for proper burial and mourning rites, I did not know that others were thinking along the same lines. Today is not exactly the first of a month or even a week-long period of mourning and remembrance rites but I am glad that it is being commemorated at the United Nations. It should go global, actively observed in the whole world, because the modern, to the extent that it has been shaped by capitalism, is a consequence of slave trade and plantation slavery.

The economic consequences are obvious: the most-developed countries in the West are largely those whose modernity is rooted in transatlantic slave trade and plantation slavery. The African body was a commodity; and its manpower, unpaid-for resource for at least 400 years. Plantation slavery morphed into colonial slavery in which, once again, African human and natural resources were cheap commodities for the colonialist buyer who determined the price and worth of that which he was buying. Don't we see echoes of that today in the unequal trade practices where the West still determines the price and worth of what it gets from Africa as well as what it sells to Africa? Colonial slavery has morphed into debt slavery. It's not an accident that the major slaving states were also the major colonial potentates, just as today they are the major creditory states.

The other side of the same coin is the undeniable fact that the victims of the slave trade and slavery on the African continent and abroad are collectively the ones experiencing underdevelopment. For example, Haiti in the eighteenth century was the economic mainstay of France, coveted by the major European powers of the time; today it is the most economically deprived country in the Western world. Haiti's story is also that of Africa and African people as a whole. The majority of the homeless in the world still come from communities that were the victims of slave trade and plantation slavery.

What was a gain for the world, especially the West, was a corresponding loss for Africa. Here I am not talking simply about the loss of human lives, power, resources—

the economic loss for Africa and the corresponding gain for the West: the slave trade and slavery were a historical trauma whose consequences for the African psyche have never been properly explored. So while the economic con sequences for both Africa and the West are obvious, the moral consequences may not be that apparent.

Gabriele Schwab,[1] extending the thought of Sigmund Freud and Nicholas Abraham and Maria Torok,[2] has argued that a person who perpetrates trauma and the person who experiences it can often shut the trauma in a psychic tomb, acting as if it never happened. The recipient does not mourn the loss and the perpetrator does not acknowledge the crime, for you cannot mourn a loss or acknowledge a crime you deny. This can occur at a community level, where horrors enacted upon a group are kept in a collective psychic tomb, their reception and perpetration passed on in silence. This, of course, means that there is no real closure and the wound festers inside to haunt the future.

The West has never properly acknowledged slavery as a crime against humanity, for to acknowledge it is to accept responsibility for the crime and its consequences. This has left a gaping wound in the collective psyche. America, for instance, was founded and built on the contradictory ideals of freedom and slavery. Many fled to freedom from persecution and religious intolerance on the European continent. But then they killed the natives and put Africans in chains. Slaves were the real founding fathers and mothers of modern America. More than 200 years of free labour, a period that saw Britain and Europe rise to industrial wealth and power—princely palaces on plantation prisons—have helped normalize a view of progress and development as the construction of a glossy middle class on the backs of a majority of poor, at home and abroad. The ethical imperative at the core is the notion that health is health only if it is rooted in the illness of another; palaces are so only when erected on prisons. It's an ethical view satirically expressed in Kenneth Grahame's *Wind in the Willows* (1908) in the character of Mole who says, 'After all, the best part of a holiday is perhaps not so much to be resting yourself, as to see all the other fellows busy working.'[3] They strive to make labour less free to approximate the slave ideal of an unfettered freedom for capital. The opposite, labour's drive for equality with capital at least, is also true. The struggle between the two tendencies is still the underlying force in the politics and culture of the world today.

The absolute unfreedom of labour, which is slavery and its various colonial and class mutations, has always been maintained by the sword, more nakedly so when labour is that of another nation or race. For North America, it was the killing of Native Americans on a scale that made David Stannard describe it as an American holocaust. This is how the West was won. For Europeans, principally the Germans, the British, the French, the Belgians, the Dutch, the Italians, the Portuguese and the

Spanish, it was colonial genocide—from Belgium's butchery of millions in the Congo, Germany's Herero horror, France's bloody orgy in Algiers and massacres in Malagasy to Britain's Mau Mau massacres and mass incarcerations. This is how democracy was exported.

The large-scale massacres and wanton genocide, enabled by mechanized armaments, has also helped normalize the hoarding of weapons of mass destruction as an expression of prosperity, power, prestige and pride, and the accompanying 'moral' horror that others dare try a similar self-projection of power and pride. De Gaulle celebrated France's nuclear explosions with the claim that, since that morning, France had become stronger and prouder. Prouder that it had acquired the capacity to annihilate humanity? It's worth noting that three of the five leading hoarders of weapons of mass destruction, the US, Britain and France, have slave-owning pasts, while the fourth, Russia, has an internal slave-owning past. Africa is the only continent where two states, South Africa and Libya, have voluntarily dismantled nuclear programmes. And yet Africa has been the recipient of nuclear tests: France in Algerian Sahara, in the midst of the anticolonial Algerian War; and, allegedly, Israel, in cooperation with apartheid South Africa, in the Prince Edward Islands. The names that the various nations have given to nuclear tests show these nations' sheer moral insensitivity to the horror they have been unleashing. Britain called their first test Hurricane, carried out in the former colony Australia; US: Trinity, carried out in the Mexican desert; Russia: Pervya Molniya, Fast Lightning; Israel: the South Atlantic Flash; and India: Smiling Buddha. France called their own after the Sahara desert rodent. Hurricane, flash, lightning, smiling, rodent—you would think that they were celebrating nature instead of the human capacity to snuff out life.

A proper mourning of the slave trade and slavery, the very foundation of modern capitalism, may well remind people about the origins of this moral perversion of casting the possibilities for mass death on a global scale as a matter of pride, while putting a smiling face on evil.

Modern Western leadership doggedly refuses to apologize for slavery, even ridiculing those who call for reparations. A prominent apologist for the slave past even suggests that the victims of the crime should actually pay reparations to the nations that enslaved them.[4] It's reminiscent of the slaves being made to compensate the slave holder for the loss he would suffer under the emancipation of labour. One can, of course, see why the perpetrators of a crime and their paid apologists may want to forget it: uneasy lies the crown on the heads of those who have committed crimes against humanity, but should the victims and their offsprings ever forget it? At the very least, we should always remember, and even draw inspiration from, those who resisted, those who always dreamt for a future without slavery and fought for it. Americans, who are so proud of their Declaration of Independence, conveniently forget that the first cry and eloquent call for freedom was uttered by the enslaved in the slave plantation.

Postcolonial Africa has also never properly mourned this trauma on its own continent nor in its diasporic communities in the Caribbean and the Americas. In Africa and the world, the slave trade and plantation slavery have never been accepted in body and mind for what they were: crimes against humanity on an unprecedented historical and geographic magnitude, a Hitlerism long before Hitler, to borrow the phraseology from Aimé Césaire's *Discourse on Colonialism* (1950). Africans may want to forget that sections of their communities cooperated in the enslavement of others; and for the Arabic-speaking North, or the Middle East, they may want to forget their role in the Arab enslavement of black Africans.

But just as there are negative moral consequences on the perpetrator of unacknowledged trauma, there are some on the recipients of the same. One of these is the negative perception of Africa and Africans by others, and the equally negative self-conception of Africa and Africans by Africans themselves. These two conceptions have common ground in the devaluation of African lives. Massacres and genocide can happen in Africa, as in the case of Rwanda, with the world looking on. With a shrug of the shoulders, they mutter: It has happened before, so what! African governments can mow down their people and go to bed and sleep soundly as if nothing has happened; politicians who settle political disputes by inciting ethnic cleansing (and counter–ethnic cleansing) can go to sleep with consciences undisturbed by what they have brought about. The colonialist did it, pitting community against community—why can't we?

Any loss of life is of course horrifying. But we have seen how frantic the world and Africa become, and rightly so, if a white European hostage is missing or meets his death in Africa. But we don't see the same when it is a case of even 100 Africans missing. It shows an indifference towards the descendants of slaves and deep concern for the descendants of slave owners. I don't advocate an equality of unconcern but, rather, call for an equality of concern.

There should be proper mourning rites for the victims and proper acknowledgement of the crime by its perpetrators. But this means learning from what happened. The slave lost the sovereignty of his body, lost control of the power of his labour and lost his language. And today, in Africa, how much control do we have over our own resources? Divisions among Africans manipulated by the divide-and-conquer tactics of the raiders helped in the enslavement process by weakening the resistance. Today, the same divisions between and within African countries continue to weaken the continent. Fake religious wars are mounted. Neo-imperialism has somehow found a way of convincing some that the problem is not imperialism but that some in Africa espouse Christian faith and others

Islam. In the name of faith, they become a willing auxiliary army of Western imperialism. There are many questions that we should ask if we have the desire to read from the tea-leaves of our history.

More important, we can learn from the 'fight-back' culture and practices of the enslaved. For instance, while today's Africa loses its languages willingly, the enslaved African lost his language unwillingly, often fighting back to create new languages out of the memory of those they were forced to give up. Denied their languages, they created new ones and made the best with that. Pan-Africanism was born in the diaspora; the new African in the Caribbean and the Americas could look back at the African continent and see it in its oneness, not in its divisions. Their cultural achievements, by way of literature and music, are monumental, and have made an indelible mark on global culture.

The world—Africa included—needs to learn from its past. Only by acknowledging the crimes committed, marked by proper mourning rites, can there come about the wholeness and the healing that the world needs so much. I hope that this day is only the beginning of the collective journey towards that 'wholiness'.

Notes

1 See Gabriele Schwab, *Haunting Legacies: Violent Histories and Transgenerational Trauma* (New York: Columbia University Press, 2010).

2 See Nicholas Abraham and Maria Torok, *The Shell and the Kernel: Renewals of Psychoanalysis*, VOL. 1 (Nicholas T. Rand ed., trans. and introd.) (Chicago: University of Chicago Press, 1994).

3 Kenneth Grahame, *The Wind in the Willows* (New York: Dover, 1999[1908]), p. 2.

4 See Dinesh D'Souza, *What's So Great about America* (Washington DC: Regnery Publishing, 2002).

NUCLEAR-ARMED CLUBSMEN

Weapons of Mass Destruction
and the Intellectual

There is an intellectual dimension to every human enterprise. The transition of the human being from fruit gatherer and hunter to farmer and domesticator of animals must have been a great leap in the conceptual relation of the human to nature. I assume that this leap was not a result of one person theorizing the concept of farming and domestication and another person putting the concept into practice. The thought and practice were one. The farmer was also the thinker. It is fairly accepted that intellectualizing as an autonomous area of human activity rose with greater material productivity and class differentiation to allow for the survival of the producer of the non-material.

Intellectuals are workers in ideas who use words as the primary means of production but they cannot eat or drink the products, much less clothe themselves with them. Words, their sound and sound quality, their arrangement and causal relation to one another, their meaning, their being as languages are especially important to that category of intellectuals who deal with the literary production and dissemination of images. They exploit every semantic, semiotic, pragmatic and syntactic aspect of words in the making of images. Like all other intellectuals, they want to show connections between phenomena.

Every imaginative act embodies a viewpoint, and the intellectual as a conjuror of images wants to persuade us to view the world and our place in it in a certain way. While viewpoint is inherent in many an intellectual product, it's more so in the work of the literary intellectual. An intellectual, however, does not work in a condition of absolute autonomy. An intellectual does not invent words, except for the occasional special need, but, rather, uses words that are inherited as language already in use. The language already in use and the contemporary historical moment mould the intellectual. It's in the context already given that the intellectual wrestles with ideas and explores images to his or her satisfaction. An intellectual has to do that—the logic of his calling—but, even then, there is an ethical dimension to intellectual production.

In May 2005, I joined 20 other intellectuals from around the world in South Korea for the Second Seoul International Forum for Literature organized on the theme of writing for peace. It made me recall the International Literature Conference in Cologne, West Germany, in August 1982, where I joined the late Heinrich Böll and other leading writers, again from around the world, to debate the same subject. It did not escape me that both conferences took place in countries divided by the same historical event. Following the Second World War, Germany was divided into East and West; following the consequences of the same war, Korea was divided into North and South. The organizers of the two conferences obviously assumed that intellectuals had something they could contribute to the issue of world peace embodied in the tensions inherent in the division of their countries.

A highlight of the get-together in Seoul was a visit to Panmunjom, 'the "truce village" that straddles the border between North and South Korea in the middle of the Demilitarized Zone'. Standing beside Kenzaburo Oe, the 1994 Nobel laureate for literature, watching the North and South Korean soldiers facing each other in hostile but poker-faced postures, I realized just how much the grounds on which we stood were a metaphor for the twentieth and twenty-first centuries. The layers of images in this place tell the history of our times: the bomb, colonialism, decolonization, neocolonialism, the Cold War, superpower rivalries and globalization. Among the intellectuals was Tibor Meray, a Hungarian journalist now living in France who was present at the signing of the armistice in a tent through which ran the boundary between North and South Korea. He was returning to the site for the first time, and he regaled us with stories and showed us pictures he had taken of the tent in the 1950s. Where the tent was once located now stood stone buildings, but the same boundary ran through a table in the bungalow where officials of both sides still met to settle disputes. Meray intrigued me, for he was a living witness and an embodiment of a history that told the same unending story. It seemed remote, yet my own intellectual development is framed by that history.

I was born under the shadow of the atomic bomb. I remember a verse in a call-and-response dance movement by some Kenyan youths of the latter half of the 1940s in which the soloist talks of his return from Japan, where he had just dropped bombs. The reference was clearly to the atomic bombs in Nagasaki and Hiroshima, but I don't know if the dancers were identifying with the act or simply recording a momentous event in human history. The horror of what the youths were singing struck me when, years later at a 1974 conference held in Tokyo on democracy and the reunification of Korea, I visited Hiroshima and saw the scene of devastation. The images and the stories of continued disastrous radioactive effects on generations born years after Hiroshima made me recall the words of the scientific director of the Manhattan Project, J. Robert Oppenheimer, who oversaw the birth of the ultimate weapon of mass destruction. Seeing the 'Trinity' test explosion at the Alamogordo test range in a desert appropriately called Jornada del Muerto (Journey of the Deadman) in New Mexico on 16 July 1945, Oppenheimer borrowed from the Bhagavadgita to describe the result of what his assembly of scientists had produced: 'I am become Death, the destroyer of worlds.'[1] Within a month, the human angels of this death visited Hiroshima and Nagasaki with the devastating effects that I could see and feel 30 years after the bombing. 'We knew the world would not be the same,' Oppenheimer had said.

How right he was: never in the history of the world had there been a man-made invention that could, at the push of a button, destroy all life on earth. More than the birth of great religious leaders, the birth of the bomb marks the severest break in the continuity of human history. There is the world before the bomb and the world after. Capitalist modernity ends with the bomb; post-modernity begins with the bomb. And we hope it will not end with the bomb.

Yes, only hope! A handful of nations now have the capacity to bombard the world over and over again. They form a nuclear club. Despite the end of the Cold War, the world is still under the shadow of sudden death. You would think that the whole world would be mobilizing to stop this shadow of death from destroying all human life, but it seems to me that the world's focus has shifted to those nations that do not have nuclear weapons, as if

NGŨGĨ WA THIONG'O

the intention of possessing nuclear arms is more dangerous than the actual possession of them. The nations that
already carry death want to convince the world that the
real threat to life lies with those who are seeking to join
their nuclear club.

Surely, non-proliferation should go hand in hand
with nuclear disarmament. Every call for nations not to
develop their own nuclear arsenals should be accompanied by an equally vehement call for nuclear nations to
disarm. One of the greatest mass movements in postwar
Britain was the campaign for nuclear disarmament. Many
members of the Labour Party—including some of its
leaders, such as Neil Kinnock—were active participants.
It is a pity that, after the party's defeat by Margaret
Thatcher, there has largely been silence on this issue in
the streets of London.

If one role of the intellectual is to use words in
defence of human life, in our times this responsibility
should translate into raising a hue and cry against the
'destroyers' of the world. Belief in stability built on
mutual assured destruction is pure madness. The first
right of any claim to intellectual life is the right to life. It
is in that spirit that the intellectuals who met in Cologne
in 1982 and in Seoul in 2005 could rightly justify their
claim to speak on issues of war and peace. In the poem
'Not What Was Meant', Bertolt Brecht writes:

Even the narrowest minds
In which peace is harbored

Are more welcome to the arts than the art lover
Who is also a lover of the art of war.[2]

The same period that saw the birth of the bomb saw
other death threats to social life. The hope generated by
the intensified decolonization that took place after the
Second World War, which led to the independence, civil
rights and social rights of many nations and communities
all over the world, was stifled by the rivalries of the Cold
War and by the emergence of the instruments for economic globalization: the Bretton Woods system, the institutions of the World Bank, the IMF and the WTO. The
Cold War is officially over, but globalization is expanding
at full speed.

Just as the world of nations is divided into those
who have the weapons of mass death— members of the
nuclear club—and those who don't, the world of capitalist globalization is divided into a handful of nations
brought together around the Group of Eight who pos-
sess wealth and the majority who live in poverty. This
is not a case of 'East is East and West is West, and never
the twain shall meet.' In fact, the wealth of this minority
of nations is rooted in the poverty of the many. The
minority who have do not consume resources solely
within their national boundaries; they use up over 90 per
cent of global human and natural resources. Alarmingly,
the gap between the two groups of nations increases
daily.

This global divide is reflected within nations, where the gap between the poor social majority and the wealthy social minority is widening. With the Dickensian world of *Oliver Twist*—'Please sir, I want some more'—reproduced in even the wealthiest of nations, the homeless, the prisoner and the beggar have become the social metaphors for our times. In eighteenth- and nineteenth-century England, the homeless who resorted to theft for survival were shipped to penal colonies, some of which later bloomed into full-fledged nations. Today the wealthy section in nations sends the homeless caught stealing to prison colonies in their territories. The prison population is the fastest-growing social sector in many nations, making Benjamin Disraeli's 'two nations' a reality in many countries. In my view, the rifts *among* nations and *within* nations are equally destroyers of worlds, and it is not surprising that the nuclear wealthy nations are also among the economically wealthy. Is this correlation not yet another area of concern for the intellectual?

Once again Brecht comes to mind. In the poem 'Speech to Danish Working-Class Actors on the Art of Observation', he calls on the workers to use their learning and teaching to play their part in all the struggles:

Of men and women of your time, thereby
Helping, with the seriousness of study and the
    cheerfulness of knowledge,
To turn the struggle into common experience and
Justice into a passion.[3]

An irony of globalization is that the globe is shrinking into a village because of information technology and yet its divisions of culture have deepened. Again, in the aftermath of the Second World War, the organization of capital took a more fundamentalist form. The market and profit became God—the Father and the Son and Holy Ghost—a religious tendency best captured by Thatcher's TINAism. The World Bank and the IMF became temples that decided on the admission and excommunication of members, and the WTO took on the role of the economic policeman.

This capitalist fundamentalism has generated other fundamentalisms in alliance with it, such as some elements of Christian fundamentalism popularly known as the Christian Right or, in opposition to it, some elements of Islamic fundamentalism, popularly viewed as terrorism. It is worth noting that the leaders of an endlessly self-righteous West have often been quite happy to work with Islamic and Christian fundamentalists when it has suited them. Otherwise, the cultural divide of 'my god is more of a god than your god' makes conversation very difficult and divides people unnecessarily. When each side claims to take orders from that side's god, the anxiety of who possesses the means of death is heightened. Claims that my god is more of a god than your god are very ungodly.

The religious ideology of capitalist fundamentalism demands the destruction of state barriers to the movement of finance capital but the erection of barriers to the

movement of labour. Democracy becomes confused with
the right of capital to move freely within and across states
but not the right of labour to do the same. Racism, which
also takes the extreme form of religious bigotry through
the boast 'my race is the chosen race,' has become more
pronounced, and, as a result, some countries are even
calling for the erection of physical barriers around their
territories. A variant of the notion of the chosen is that of
exceptionalism. What if every nation saw itself as excep-
tional and not subject to norms that regulate relations
between nations and peoples? Ethnic cleansing in nation-
states becomes the occasion for massacre and genocide.

In a world with barriers to contact and barriers to
speech, there must still be a place for those saying that
the essence of the word is to talk, to make conversation,
and that, without conversation, communication, the
human community would never have come to be. We
would have remained like all the other components of
nature, undifferentiated from it, in perpetual repetition
of its same cycles. Nurture out of nature is enabled by the
word as language. The role of the word is to connect, as
defined in E. M. Forster's *Howards End* (1910): 'Only
connect! That was the whole of her sermon. Only connect the prose and the passion, and both will be exalted,
and human love will be seen at its height. Live in fragments no longer. Only connect, and the beast and the
monk, robbed of the isolation that is life to either, will
die.'[4] John Donne expresses the same idea in 'Meditation

XVII' (1624).Unfortunately there are many who still think they can profit best in a life lived in fragments of nations, race, gender, religion, especially when they can claim that their fragment is 'wholier' than others

This human connection Donne proclaims should surely be truer of cultures. All cultures are tributaries to the common pool of human experience. The death of any culture diminishes me because it is one tributary less for the human community. We only have to connect, to help put faiths and doctrines and languages, big or small, into dialogue. And if, in this connection, I quote Cesaire, it is because what he says of culture contact was our organizing motto at the International Center for Writing and Translation at the University of California, Irvine. In his castigation of colonialism, he admits: 'It is a good thing to place different civilizations into contact with each other; that it is an excellent thing to blend different worlds; that whatever its own particular genius may be, a civilization that withdraws into itself atrophies; that for civilization, exchange is oxygen.'[5]

It is difficult to prescribe any one role for the intellectual. Intellectuals can and must explore all possibilities and logical implications of their chosen fields and form. But I hope that the intellectuals of our times believe in the contact of cultures as the oxygen of the human community; that in the struggle for peace and nuclear disarmament, for social justice and for cultural exchange, today's intellectuals can find what they need to further facilitate the generation of more oxygen, thus enabling a shared human inheritance of the best in all faiths, doctrines, cultures and languages.

Unfortunately, in the academy, I have seen a tendency to shy away from engagement with words like freedom, liberation, social justice, peace, nuclear disarmament, class struggle, commitment and a retreat into a modern scholasticism where splitting hairs about form takes precedence over content. In eschewing those words, the academy leaves them to the forces that would like to empty them of content, relevance and meaningful reference. Emily Dickinson says, 'A Word that breathes distinctly / Has not the power to die.'[6]

Political authoritarianism is terrified of the power of the word that has become flesh. It loves the word that has been dislodged from the flesh. The challenge for the intellectual is to make words become flesh, to make them breathe distinctly. Theory must always return to the earth to get recharged. For the word that breathes life is still needed to challenge the one that carries death and devastation. Works of imagination and critical theories can only weaken themselves by pulling back from that challenge.

Notes

1   J. Robert Oppenheimer, '"Now I Am Become Death ..."' (available at. http://www.atomicarchive.com/-Movies/Movie8.shtml; last accessed on 16 April 2015).

2   Bertolt Brecht, 'Not What Was Meant' (Frank Jones trans.) in *Poems, 1913–56* (John Willet and Ralph Manheim eds) (London: Methuen, 1976), pp. 437–8; here, p. 438.

3   Bertolt Brecht, 'Speech to Danish Working-Class Actors on the Art of Observation' (John Willett trans.) in ibid., pp. 233–8; here, p. 238.

4   E. M. Forster, *Howards End* (New York: Barnes and Noble, 1993[1910]), p. 157.

5   Aimé Cesaire, *Discourse on Colonialism* (New York: Monthly Review Press, 2000[1950]), p. 33.

6   Emily Dickinson, 'Poem, 1651' in *The Complete Poems of Emily Dickinson* (Thomas H. Johnson ed.) (Boston: Little, Brown, 1960), pp. 675–6; here, p. 676.

WRITING FOR PEACE

Or, the Two Rifts Revisited

As a writer, and more so as a writer from Kenya, Africa, I cannot be indifferent to the issues of peace and war. My father escaped conscription into the First World War by faking an illness. Whenever he went for a medical exam, he would chew some herbs to raise his body temperature. Hundreds of African conscripts died in the German East African campaign against the British. If he had gone to that war, he might have met the same fate and I might never have been born. As it is, I was born in 1938, at the start of the Second World War in which I was later to lose my brother, a British soldier fighting for the King, as they used to sing. The war ended only to see Kenya plunge into another war, this time, a war of anti-colonial resistance to end the British settler occupation of more than 50 years. This was the Mau Mau War that broke out in 1952, during the same period as the Korean War. Independence came in 1963 but it was an independence that came in the midst of the Cold War that made many of the newly independent African countries become battlegrounds for the East and the West.

Still we were full of hope at what then looked like the dawn of a new era in Africa and the world. There were a few warnings that all was not well and it may have been these that prompted me, as a young writer, in fact, then just a college student, to write a paper entitled 'Kenya: The Two Rifts', which was published in the *New African*, a new literary journal, in the September issue of 1962.

In the paper, I argued that the new Kenya, like many African countries, had to find a way of overcoming two rifts that I then saw as undermining the stability of new independence. There was a possible rift between the ethnicities that made up the country, often rooted in uneven regional development, a heritage of colonial practices. But I saw another rift, which later became the subject of my fiction, between the new elite who wielded power and the general population, particularly the working majority. I wrote as if these rifts were obvious and hoped that we would develop an economy, political practices, cultural values and pragmatic policies that would narrow the two rifts.

Looking back, I am not so sure, as far as the two divisions are concerned, whether the world of my childhood was all that different from the world of my children today. True, the colonial world is a thing of the past. The Cold War that saw so many dictatorships thrive, largely because they were supported by the West and seen as loyal allies, is also in the past, at least in form. And the world has seen the most incredible feats of achievement thanks to new technologies that make production for a fully fed, fully clothed and fully housed world possible. Human adventures and breakthroughs in space are also breathtaking. From the point of view of those travellers in space, our earth is truly one. Information technology is also bringing the world together, making regions hitherto removed from one another look like neighbourhoods.

But the world, seemingly on the verge of a breakthrough in terms of what is possible for uniting humans, is threatened by the two rifts that I wrote about in 1962, which have now become a global phenomenon. I am concerned that in the economic, political and cultural map of the world, a handful of Western nations control over 90 per cent of world resources, both human and natural. The world is indeed divided between a handful of creditor nations and hundreds of debtor nations. The irony is that through debts and debt servicing, these poor nations have become net exporters of the capital they so desperately need for their own development. The gap between the wealth of a few Have nations, largely grouped around G8, and the poverty of Have-Not nations, largely located in Africa, Asia and South America, is increasing.

What is alarming is not only the existence of the two divisions between and within nations but also the growing culture of their acceptance as norms, even desirable at times as the inevitable consequences of progress and modernity. The result is inverted values. Humans are there for progress but progress is not there for them. We are creating a world in which capital has the freedom to move quickly across the borders of nation-states, even making a mockery of such borders, but we erect racist barriers to the movement of labour. In a world that looks as if it is increasingly becoming one, racist and ethnic intolerance has increased. Is it any wonder that there have been massacres of innocents in the name of ethnic cleansing?

There is an increasing deification of the market as the sole arbiter of human economic practices. The deity shows pleasure to his true worshippers by increasing their profit and displeasure by withholding profits. The deity has even disowned all his other sons and daughters and left only one—a most intolerant capitalism. The IMF, the World Bank and even the WTO have become temples and those who depart from the tents of worship are excommunicated. Capitalist fundamentalism and the forces it unleashes becomes a threat to the very modernity its earlier more tolerant form had created. Fundamentalism is when a system—any system —claims that there is only one way of performance, and, in this case, the market seems to say that there is only one way of worshipping it, through privatization and the abandonment of any social control to the practice of capital.

I see the two divisions creating a very unbalanced world, a very dangerous world, a very unstable world— for when nations, big and small, refuse to address and confront the two divisions, they are very busy looking for causes of national and global instability elsewhere.

There are two potential responses to the possibilities of peace in the context of the two divisions. There is the conservative approach: peace through the preservation of the status quo. This is 'peace' erected on slavery and it is peace only to the oppressing class or nation. The absurdity of this approach to peace was best articulated by Leo Tolstoy when he talked of the man who is carried on another's back and who will vehemently protest his willingness to do everything to help his victim—everything, that is, except getting off his back. The advocates of mere aid-giving are in this category. The basic question is not that of aid or lack of aid to the underdeveloped world, but that of getting off their backs so they can develop a national base for their economy, politics and culture and from which they can interact with other nations and peoples.

Then there is the radical response. This calls for a total transformation of the systems of inequality and oppression in every nation and between all nations. Modern industry, science and technology, were they not directed towards maintaining inequalities (imagine the billions spent on nuclear and conventional arms!), could transform the lives of millions on earth. As it is, we are now in a world of contradictions. Human technology and ingenuity has created an endless frontier in space as well as life in genetics, and yet human greed has decreed that there be poverty and disease on earth. We have the means to save life and yet we sit on heaps of weapons of mass destruction, pointing an accusing finger at everyone else but ourselves. Poverty between and within nations is no less a weapon of mass dissatisfaction. Insecurity haunts the streets of even the most heavily armed nation. I, myself, do not believe that peace is possible in an imperialist-dominated world or a world in which prison population is the fastest-growing sector in the wealthiest of nations.

Literature provides us with images of the world in which we live. These images shape our consciousness to look at the world in a certain way. Our propensity to action or inaction or a certain kind of action or inaction can be profoundly affected by the way we look at the world. Writing for peace should, at the very least, mean raising human consciousness to an uncompromising hatred of all exploitative, parasitic relations between nations and between peoples within each nation. The struggle should be for a world in which one's cleanliness is not dependent on another's dirt, one's health on another's frailty and one's welfare on another's misery. Peace is only possible in a world in which the condition of the development of any one nation is the development of all. Globalization of greed and the means of human destruction should be met with the globalism of the creed of sanity and human creativity. Now more than ever in human history, communities of different races, faiths, cultures need to talk, to claim responsibility for their common future rooted in the notion of the sovereignty of the people of the earth.

Writing for peace should mean a constant reminder to humans that we live on the same earth and that any stockpile of weapons of mass destruction by any nation, big or small, is an act of war against the future of humanity. Let all nations turn those weapons into ploughshares. The earth is our communal father and mother as well as our future, and peace is the only guarantor of that common future, our common dream.

BIBLIOGRAPHY

ABRAHAM, Nicholas, and Maria Torok, *The Shell and the Kernel: Renewals of Psychoanalysis*, VOL. 1 (Nicholas T. Rand ed., trans. and introd.). Chicago: University of Chicago Press, 1994.

ACHEBE, Chinua. *Anthills of the Savannah*. New York: Anchor-Doubleday, 1988.

BÉTI, Mongo. *The Poor Christ of Bomba* (Gerald Moore trans.). London: Heinemann, 1971. Originally: *Le pauvre Christ de Bomba*. Paris: Laffont, 1956.

BRECHT, Bertolt. *The Caucasian Chalk Circle* (Stephan S. Brecht trans., with W. H. Auden). Oxford: Heinemann, 1976. Originally: *Der Kaukasische Kreidekreis*. Frankfurt-am-Main: Suhrkamp, 1955.

———. 'Not What Was Meant' (Frank Jones trans.) in *Poems, 1913–56* (John Willet and Ralph Manheim eds). London: Methuen, 1976, pp. 437–8.

———. 'Speech to Danish Working-Class Actors on the Art of Observation' (John Willett trans.) in *Poems, 1913–56* (John Willet and Ralph Manheim eds). London: Methuen, 1976, pp. 233–8.

CÉSAIRE, Aimé. *Discourse on Colonialism* (Joan Pinkham trans.). New York: Monthly Review Press, 1972. Originally: *Discours sur le colonialisme*. Paris: Editions Présence Africaines, 1955.

DICKINSON, Emily. 'Poem, 1651' in *The Complete Poems of Emily Dickinson* (Thomas H. Johnson ed.). Boston: Little, Brown, 1960, pp. 675–6.

DIOP, Cheikh Anta. 'When Can We Talk of an African Renaissance' (1948) in *Towards the African Renaissance: Essays in African Culture and Development, 1946–1960* (Egbuna P. Modum trans.). London: Karnak House, 1996, p. 33–46.

D'SOUZA, Dinesh. *What's So Great about America*. Washington DC: Regnery Publishing, 2002.

EZE, Emmanuel Chukwudi. 'The Color of Reason: The Idea of "Race" in Kant's Anthropology' in Emmanuel Chukwudi Eze (ed.), *Postcolonial African Philosophy: A Critical Reader*. Oxford: Blackwell, pp. 103–40.

FANON, Frantz. *Black Skin, White Masks* (Richard Philcox trans.). New York: Grove Press, 2008. Originally: *Peau noire, masques blancs*. Paris: Éditions du Seuil, 1952.

———. *The Wretched of the Earth* (Richard Philcox trans.). New York: Grove Press, 2004. Originally: *La damnés de la terre*. Paris: François Maspero éditeur, 1961.

FORSTER, E. M. *Howards End*. New York: Barnes and Noble, 1993[1910].

FOUCAULT, Michel. *Discipline and Punish: The Birth of the Prison* (Alan Sheridan trans.). New York: Vintage, 1995.

GRAHAME, Kenneth. *The Wind in the Willows*. New York: Dover, 1999[1908].

KENYATTA, Jomo. *Facing Mount Kenya: The Tribal Life of the Gikuyu*. London: Vintage, 1965[1938].

LENIN, V. I. *Imperialism: The Highest Stage of Capitalism*. London: Penguin, 2010[1916].

MARX, Karl, and Friedrich Engels. *The Communist Manifesto*. New York: Simon and Schuster, 1964[1848].

MILLS, Bronwyn. 'Caribbean Cartographies: Maps, Cosmograms, and the Caribbean Imagination'. Unpublished PhD dissertation, Department of Comparative Literature, New York University, New York, 2004.

MITTLEMAN, James H. 'Alternative Globalization' in Richard Sandbrook (ed.), *Civilizing Globalization*. New York: State University of New York Press, 2003, pp. 237–52.

NGŨGĨ wa Thiong'o. *Decolonizing the Mind: The Politics of Language in African Litearure*. Nairobi: East African Educational Publishers, 1986.

———. *A Grain of Wheat*. Johannesburg: Heinemann, 1967.

———. *Matigari*. Johannesburg: Heinemann, 1987.

———. *Moving the Center: The Struggle for Cultural Freedoms*. Oxford: James Currey / Nairobi: East African Educational Publishers, 1993.

———. *Penpoints, Gunpoints and Dreams: Towards a Critical Theory of the Arts and the State in Africa; Clarendon Lectures in English Literature, 1996*. Oxford: Clarendon, 1998.

———. *Petals of Blood*. Johannesburg: Heinemann, 1977.

———. *Something Torn and New: An African Renaissance*. New York: BasicCivitas Books, 2009.

———. *Wizard of the Crow*. London: Vintage, 2006

——— and Ngũgĩ wa Mĩriĩ. *I Will Marry When I Want*. Johannesburg: Heinemann, 1980.

NKRUMAH, Kwame. *Africa Must Unite*. Johannesburg: Heinemann, 1963.

———. *Neo-colonialism: The Last Stage of Imperialism*. London: Nelson, 1965.

PATON, Alan. *Cry, the Beloved Country*. New York: Scribner, 1987[1948].

POLANYI, Karl . *The Great Transformation*. Boston, MA: Beacon Press, 1944.

SCHWAB, Gabriele. *Haunting Legacies: Violent Histories and Transgenerational Trauma*. New York: Columbia University Press, 2010.

SHAKESPEARE, William. *Julius Caesar* in *Complete Works* (W. J. Craig ed.). Oxford: Oxford University Press, 1943, pp. 820–45.

———. *King Lear* in *Complete Works* (W. J. Craig ed.). Oxford: Oxford University Press, 1943, pp. 908–42.

STANNARD, David. *American Holocaust: The Conquest of the New World*. New York: Oxford University Press, 1992.

TUCKER, Robert C. (ed.). *The Marx–Engels Reader*, 2ND EDN. New York: W. W. Norton, 1978.

WILLIAMS, Eric. *Capitalism and Slavery*. Richmond, VA: University of North Carolina Press, 1944.

MARYSE CONDÉ

The Journey of a Caribbean Writer
Translated by Richard Philcox

2014 | Cloth | 5" x 8.5" | 220 pages | $25
ISBN 978 0 8574 2 097 8

In this collection of essays and lectures, Maryse Condé reflects on the ideas and histories that have moved her. From the use of French as her literary language to the agonies of the Middle Passage, at the horrors of African dictatorship, and the politically induced poverty of the Caribbean to migration under globalization, Condé casts her unflinching eye over the world which is her inheritence.

....

RICHARD TURNER

The Eye of the Needle
Towards Participatory Democracy in South Africa
With Essays by Tony Morphet
and a New Foreword by Rosalind C. Morris

2015 | Cloth | 5" x 8" | 266 pages | $21
ISBN 978 0 8574 2 237 8

Richard Turner's most influential and incendiary text, first published in 1972, returns to print at a critical moment in South African history, when many have turned their attention once again to Black Consciousness and a reconsideration of the Durban Moment. Accompanied by Tony Morphet's contextualizing essays, this is an excellent entry point for both historical reflection on 1970s South Africa and critical engagement with social justice.

WILLIAM KENTRIDGE AND ROSALIND C. MORRIS

That Which Is Not Drawn
Conversations

2013 | Cloth | 5.5" x 7.75" | 200 pages | $35
ISBN 978 0 8574 2 175 3

For more than three decades, artist William Kentridge has explored in his work the nature of subjectivity, the possibilities of revolution, the Enlightenment's legacy in Africa, and the nature of time itself, and has stretched the boundaries of the very media he employs. This long, engaging dialogue, is a guide to the work of one of our greatest living artists.

....

WILLIAM KENTRIDGE AND ROSALIND C. MORRIS

Accounts and Drawings from Underground
The East Rand Proprietary Mines Cash Book, 1906

2015 | Cloth | 8.25" x 11" | 196 pages | 61 facsimiles | $100
ISBN 978 0 8574 2 205 7

Renowned artist William Kentridge takes the pages of the 1906 Cash Book of the East Rand Proprietary Mines Corporation and transforms it into something wholly new through 40 landscape drawings as a visual epitaph to a history of disappearances; anthropologist Rosalind C. Morris plumbs the text of the cash book to generate a unique narrative account—an unprecedented collaboration.

MATTHEW KENTRIDGE

The Soho Chronicles

10 Films by William Kentridge

2015 | Cloth |8.75" x 8.75" | 438 pages | Illustrated in colour throughout | Enhanced by Augmented Reality feature | $150
ISBN 978 0 8574 2 176 0

In *The Soho Chronicles*, William Kentridge's brother Matthew, who has witnessed the evolution of William's technique, themes, and ideas, shares a never-before-seen perspective on both William and his films that sheds new light on the creator and his alter ego.

....

ANTJIE KROG

Conditional Tense

*Memory and Vocabulary after the South African
Truth and Reconciliation Commission*

2013 | Cloth |5" x 8" | 344 pages | $30
ISBN 978 0 8574 2 174 6

Using the South African Truth and Reconciliation Commission as starting point, acclaimed writer Antjie Krog's essays explore texts from every corner of South Africa in an attempt to remap the borders of her country's communities. Through this extraordinary marriage of academic observation and poetic intervention, Krog tries to move South Africa beyond the present moment and towards a vocabulary of grace and care.